TORAH PORTIONS WORKBOOK
N U M B E R S

THIS WORKBOOK BELONGS TO:

_____

Deuteronomy 6:5-9 "Love the Lord your God with all your heart, with all your soul, and with all your strength. Take to heart these words that I give you today. Repeat them to your children. Talk about them when you're at home or away, when you lie down or get up. Write them down, and tie them around your wrist, and wear them as headbands as a reminder. Write them on the door frames of your houses and on your gates."

Deuteronomy 4:9-10 "But watch out! Be careful never to forget what you yourself have seen. Do not let these memories escape from your mind as long as you live! And be sure to pass them on to your children and grandchildren. Never forget the day when you stood before the Lord your God at Mount Sinai, where he told me, Summon the people before me, and I will personally instruct them. Then they will learn to fear me as long as they live, and they will teach their children to fear me also."

Deuteronomy 11:19 Teach them to your children. "Talk about them when you are at home and when you are on the road, when you are going to bed and when you are getting up."

Matthew 19:13-15 "One day some parents brought their children to Yeshua so he could lay his hands on them and pray for them. But the disciples scolded the parents for bothering him. But Yeshua said, "Let the children come to me. Don't stop them! For the Kingdom of Heaven belongs to those who are like these children." And he placed his hands on their heads and blessed them before he left."

Proverbs 20:11 "Even a child makes himself known by his doings, whether his work is pure, and whether it is right."

Proverbs 22:6 "Train up a child in the way he should go: and when he is old, he will not depart from it. "

We can all agree that we see things around us changing rapidly as the "end times" are nearing. We see that in order for our children to be spiritually grounded in their faith and able to fight the spiritual battles that lay ahead they need to be prepared.

We would all like to be able to shelter our children from what lies ahead and protect them from all the "bad" around them. But really, if we equip them with God's Word, and teach them the love of Yeshua, what better gift could we give them.

We feel strongly that to **"train up a child in the way he should go..."** they need to be present. They need to hear what the Scriptures say, and feel as if they are a part of the reason that they are going to study. They should also feel comfortable enough that if they desire to participate in a group discussion that they are able. We do understand that getting children involved has it's challenges, and this is not something that happens at one meeting. It takes time and patience on EVERYONES part. Even those who do not have children can help. We are a body of believers and all aspects of that body should be working together as a whole.

FELLOWSHIP LEADERS:

What can you do for your group to help the children want to be more involved?

- Do you give children an opportunity to read (shorter broken down segments) during meeting.
- Do you ask them for assistance in setting up chairs or distributing handouts?
- Can you come up with some more simplistic questions for children to answer during that weeks Torah portion? What was Abraham's sons name? How many of each animal was on the Arc? Etc.
- Is there a child that would like to say a prayer?

THOSE ATTENDING WITHOUT CHILDREN:

- Do you have a listening ear?
- Do you have songs to sing or stories to tell that children would like to hear?
- Could you "adopt" a child for a day? Sit with them, help them to pay attention or to listen?

OTHER SUGGESTIONS:

- **Adults:** Make "deeper" topic notes during the study/bible reading while children are present...once you are finished, excuse the children if they want to then go play or have desert. Everyone takes a short break, then if there are "deeper" things that others would like to discuss you can do that while children are playing. Not everything is child appropriate, so this will offer adults an opportunity to discuss further the scriptures or topics they desire.

- After study, commend the children that participated...tell them what a good job they did with their reading, or how much you liked their comments or prayer.

- **Children/Teens:** Encourage your child to associate with "older" ones attending.

- Encourage your child to get to know those in the group better...ask them questions about when they were kids, how were things different. What are some of their hobbies or interest?

- Is there something your child can do to help those who are elderly? Get them a drink...carry their bags to the car for them. etc.

We realize that there are many different situations and circumstances that parents and grandparents and fellowships deal with regarding this issue and nothing is black and white. Children learn in many different ways, and a 14 year old is not going to have the same interest as a 4 year old, but there are countless ways that we can incorporate our children of all ages to be present during the Bible Study. Some of these may be things you already do, but it may also be a way that we can all work together to help each other in love.

Even if your study currently does things a certain way, maybe you can offer some suggestions to the group or come up with your own ideas or ways to incorporate children into your home study. This may be a little more different than what you have done in the past or are currently doing, but if everyone has the same goal in mind, which is to bring up our children to a deeper understanding and greater knowledge of God's word, then it will be worth it, we will have WON the battle!

Torah Town has put together this booklet as a tool to help Parents, Fellowship Leaders, and even those of the home study family that don't have children. We have tried to incorporate something for all ages and interest. We pray that this will be a blessing to everyone young and old.

And, as always, feel free to make as many copies as you need and share them with others.

To the Parents:

This workbook is designed to enhance your child's learning and participation during Your Community Fellowship Meetings and throughout the week leading up to each Sabbath. In it you will find many activities for each parsha segment, including verses from the Prophets and the New Testament that we pray will both stimulate the mind and keep little hands busy.

You will find each Torah Portion is broken down into daily readings. You may decide on using the Torah Portions in this book as a homeschooling tool. The World English Bible (WEB) is used throughout and we have changed Yahweh to YHWH to allow for your personal interpretation of the Name. We chose this version since it is easily read and can be understood by younger children.

Each Torah Portion has one or more **highlighted text** pertaining to a concept, idea or commandment, and are for spurring thought, verbal interaction and participation.

About Our Activities and Games:

MAKE A MARK – Is a listening game to see how many times someone in the assembly says certain words. This will instill good listening habits along with paying attention to the Torah Reading.

FIRST FIND – This is a Scripture Hunting game that will build knowledge of the location of Bible Books and increase participation in the Bible Study. Allow them to read the passage they find and have a special treat or small gift like scripture pencils to give to whoever finds the passage first.

COLORING PAGE – Each Coloring page is based on the weekly Torah Portion. Allow them to color while listening to the Bible Study. Children are great multi-taskers and you will be surprised at how much they absorb.

WORD FIND – Is the standard word search game where each word is based on the Parsha reading. Aimed at the older children to keep them interested in the topics presented each week.

CROSSWORD – For more advanced or older children. As with all other activities, it is based on the weekly Torah Portion, Prophets or New Testament verses for that week.

VERSE FIND – The letters are scrambled below a grid. The object is to solve in order to know the contents of the verse. (The Answer is Provided in the Title)

SCRAMBLE – Several words are scrambled and in order to solve the puzzle. Once the words are discovered, match the corresponding number with the letter to find the hidden phrase.

HIDDEN VERSE – Solve the hidden verse by finding the words in the list and then copy the remaining letters in order on the lines provided. (The Answer is Provided in the Title)

"Children are great imitators. So give them something great to imitate."

TABLE OF CONTENTS

World English Bible* used throughout
Yahweh changed to YHWH to allow for your personal interpretation of the Name

BEMIDBAR (NUMBERS)

** One week is always Passover and another is always Sukkot, and the final parashah, *V'Zot HaBerachah*, is always read on Simchat Torah. Therefore, there can be up to 53 weeks available for the other 53 portions.
In years with fewer than 53 available weeks, some readings are combined to achieve the needed number of weekly readings.

BAMIDBAR

בְּמִדְבַּר

NUMBERS

It Means: IN THE WILDERNESS

Our Thirty-Fourth Torah Portion is called Bamidbar! בְּמִדְבַּר
Numbers 1:1 – Numbers 4:20
PROPHETS: Hosea 1:10-2:23
NEW TESTAMENT: Luke 16:1-17:10; 1 Corinthians 12:12-31

MAKE A MARK
Each time you hear someone say one of the words below make a '/" beside the word. See how many marks you can get!

son	
Moses	
made	
children	
tribe	
division	

FIRST FIND

~

If someone mentions a verse or scripture that is NOT in this Torah Portion, see if YOU can be the First to Find it!

This Weeks Torah Portion is:

Parsha: _____

Scriptures: _____

Name: _____

words I didn't Understand

My Favorite Song was:

_____

date: _____

I talked to _____
about Today's Study.

The Most IMPORTANT thing I Learned today was:

MY NOTES

Draw something you learned today

I brought My Bible with me ☐
I am sitting with my Family ☐
I am ready to listen Carefully ☐

A Census of Israel's Warriors

SUNDAY Num 1:1 YHWH spoke to Moses in the wilderness of Sinai, in the Tent of Meeting, on the first day of the second month, in the second year after they had come out of the land of Egypt, saying,

Num 1:2 "Take a census of all the congregation of the children of Israel, by their families, by their fathers' houses, according to the number of the names, every male, one by one;

Num 1:3 from twenty years old and upward, all who are able to go out to war in Israel. You and Aaron shall count them by their divisions.

Num 1:4 With you there shall be a man of every tribe; everyone head of his fathers' house.

Num 1:5 These are the names of the men who shall stand with you: Of Reuben: Elizur the son of Shedeur.

Num 1:6 Of Simeon: Shelumiel the son of Zurishaddai.

Num 1:7 Of Judah: Nahshon the son of Amminadab.

Num 1:8 Of Issachar: Nethanel the son of Zuar.

Num 1:9 Of Zebulun: Eliab the son of Helon.

Num 1:10 Of the children of Joseph: Of Ephraim: Elishama the son of Ammihud. Of Manasseh: Gamaliel the son of Pedahzur.

Num 1:11 Of Benjamin: Abidan the son of Gideoni.

Num 1:12 Of Dan: Ahiezer the son of Ammishaddai.

Num 1:13 Of Asher: Pagiel the son of Ochran.

Num 1:14 Of Gad: Eliasaph the son of Deuel.

Num 1:15 Of Naphtali: Ahira the son of Enan."

Num 1:16 ***These are those who were called of the congregation, the princes of the tribes of their fathers; they were the heads of the thousands of Israel.***

Num 1:17 Moses and Aaron took these men who are mentioned by name.

Num 1:18 They assembled all the congregation together on the first day of the second month; and they declared their ancestry by their families, by their fathers' houses, according to the number of the names, from twenty years old and upward, one by one.

Num 1:19 As YHWH commanded Moses, so he counted them in the wilderness of Sinai.

MONDAY Num 1:20 The children of Reuben, Israel's firstborn, their generations, by their families, by their fathers' houses, according to the number of the names, one by one, every male from twenty years old and upward, all who were able to go out to war;

MY NOTES

Num 1:21 those who were counted of them, of the tribe of Reuben, were forty-six thousand five hundred.

Num 1:22 Of the children of Simeon, their generations, by their families, by their fathers' houses, those who were counted of it, according to the number of the names, one by one, every male from twenty years old and upward, all who were able to go out to war;

Num 1:23 those who were counted of them, of the tribe of Simeon, were fifty-nine thousand three hundred.

Num 1:24 Of the children of Gad, their generations, by their families, by their fathers' houses, according to the number of the names, from twenty years old and upward, all who were able to go out to war;

Num 1:25 those who were counted of them, of the tribe of Gad, were forty-five thousand six hundred fifty.

Num 1:26 Of the children of Judah, their generations, by their families, by their fathers' houses, according to the number of the names, from twenty years old and upward, all who were able to go out to war;

Num 1:27 those who were counted of them, of the tribe of Judah, were seventy-four thousand six hundred.

Num 1:28 Of the children of Issachar, their generations, by their families, by their fathers' houses, according to the number of the names, from twenty years old and upward, all who were able to go out to war;

Num 1:29 those who were counted of them, of the tribe of Issachar, were fifty-four thousand four hundred.

Num 1:30 Of the children of Zebulun, their generations, by their families, by their fathers' houses, according to the number of the names, from twenty years old and upward, all who were able to go out to war;

Num 1:31 those who were counted of them, of the tribe of Zebulun, were fifty-seven thousand four hundred.

Num 1:32 Of the children of Joseph, of the children of Ephraim, their generations, by their families, by their fathers' houses, according to the number of the names, from twenty years old and upward, all who were able to go out to war;

Num 1:33 those who were counted of them, of the tribe of Ephraim, were forty thousand five hundred.

Num 1:34 Of the children of Manasseh, their generations, by their families, by their fathers' houses, according to the number of the names, from twenty years old and upward, all who were able to go out to war;

Num 1:35 those who were counted of them, of the tribe of Manasseh, were thirty-two thousand two hundred.

MY NOTES

Num 1:36 Of the children of Benjamin, their generations, by their families, by their fathers' houses, according to the number of the names, from twenty years old and upward, all who were able to go out to war;

Num 1:37 those who were counted of them, of the tribe of Benjamin, were thirty-five thousand four hundred.

Num 1:38 Of the children of Dan, their generations, by their families, by their fathers' houses, according to the number of the names, from twenty years old and upward, all who were able to go out to war;

Num 1:39 those who were counted of them, of the tribe of Dan, were sixty-two thousand seven hundred.

Num 1:40 Of the children of Asher, their generations, by their families, by their fathers' houses, according to the number of the names, from twenty years old and upward, all who were able to go out to war;

Num 1:41 those who were counted of them, of the tribe of Asher, were forty-one thousand five hundred.

Num 1:42 Of the children of Naphtali, their generations, by their families, by their fathers' houses, according to the number of the names, from twenty years old and upward, all who were able to go out to war;

Num 1:43 those who were counted of them, of the tribe of Naphtali, were fifty-three thousand four hundred.

Num 1:44 These are those who were counted, whom Moses and Aaron counted, and the princes of Israel, being twelve men: they were each one for his fathers' house.

Num 1:45 So all those who were counted of the children of Israel by their fathers' houses, from twenty years old and upward, all who were able to go out to war in Israel;

Num 1:46 even all those who were counted were six hundred three thousand five hundred fifty.

Levites Exempted

Num 1:47 But the Levites after the tribe of their fathers were not counted among them.

Num 1:48 For YHWH spoke to Moses, saying,

Num 1:49 "Only the tribe of Levi you shall not count, neither shall you take a census of them among the children of Israel;

Num 1:50 **but appoint the Levites over the Tabernacle of the Testimony, and over all its furnishings, and over all that belongs to it. They shall carry the tabernacle, and all its furnishings; and they shall take care of it, and shall encamp around it.**

MY NOTES

Num 1:51 When the tabernacle is to move, the Levites shall take it down; and when the tabernacle is to be set up, the Levites shall set it up. The stranger who comes near shall be put to death.

Num 1:52 The children of Israel shall pitch their tents, every man by his own camp, and every man by his own standard, according to their divisions.

Num 1:53 But the Levites shall encamp around the Tabernacle of the Testimony, that there may be no wrath on the congregation of the children of Israel: and the Levites shall be responsible for the Tabernacle of the Testimony."

Num 1:54 Thus the children of Israel did. According to all that YHWH commanded Moses, so they did.

Arrangement of the Camp

TUESDAY Num 2:1 YHWH spoke to Moses and to Aaron, saying,

Num 2:2 *"The children of Israel shall encamp every man by his own standard, with the banners of their fathers' houses: at a distance from the Tent of Meeting shall they encamp around it."*

Num 2:3 Those who encamp on the east side toward the sunrise shall be of the standard of the camp of Judah, according to their divisions: and the prince of the children of Judah shall be Nahshon the son of Amminadab.

Num 2:4 His division, and those who were counted of them, were seventy-four thousand six hundred.

Num 2:5 Those who encamp next to him shall be the tribe of Issachar: and the prince of the children of Issachar shall be Nethanel the son of Zuar.

Num 2:6 His division, and those who were counted of it, were fifty-four thousand four hundred.

Num 2:7 The tribe of Zebulun: and the prince of the children of Zebulun shall be Eliab the son of Helon.

Num 2:8 His division, and those who were counted of it, were fifty-seven thousand four hundred.

Num 2:9 All who were counted of the camp of Judah were one hundred eighty-six thousand four hundred, according to their divisions. They shall set out first.

Num 2:10 "On the south side shall be the standard of the camp of Reuben according to their divisions. The prince of the children of Reuben shall be Elizur the son of Shedeur.

Num 2:11 His division, and those who were counted of it, were forty-six thousand five hundred.

Num 2:12 "Those who encamp next to him shall be the tribe of Simeon. The prince of the children of Simeon shall be Shelumiel the son of Zurishaddai.

MY NOTES

Num 2:13 His division, and those who were counted of them, were fifty-nine thousand three hundred.

Num 2:14 "The tribe of Gad: and the prince of the children of Gad shall be Eliasaph the son of Reuel.

Num 2:15 His division, and those who were counted of them, were forty-five thousand six hundred fifty.

Num 2:16 "All who were counted of the camp of Reuben were one hundred fifty-one thousand four hundred fifty, according to their armies. They shall set out second.

Num 2:17 "Then the Tent of Meeting shall set out, with the camp of the Levites in the middle of the camps. As they encamp, so shall they set out, every man in his place, by their standards.

Num 2:18 "On the west side shall be the standard of the camp of Ephraim according to their divisions: and the prince of the children of Ephraim shall be Elishama the son of Ammihud.

Num 2:19 His division, and those who were counted of them, were forty thousand five hundred.

Num 2:20 "Next to him shall be the tribe of Manasseh: and the prince of the children of Manasseh shall be Gamaliel the son of Pedahzur.

Num 2:21 His division, and those who were counted of them, were thirty-two thousand two hundred.

Num 2:22 "The tribe of Benjamin: and the prince of the children of Benjamin shall be Abidan the son of Gideoni.

Num 2:23 His army, and those who were counted of them, were thirty-five thousand four hundred.

Num 2:24 "All who were counted of the camp of Ephraim were one hundred eight thousand one hundred, according to their divisions. They shall set out third.

Num 2:25 "On the north side shall be the standard of the camp of Dan according to their divisions: and the prince of the children of Dan shall be Ahiezer the son of Ammishaddai.

Num 2:26 His division, and those who were counted of them, were sixty-two thousand seven hundred.

Num 2:27 "Those who encamp next to him shall be the tribe of Asher: and the prince of the children of Asher shall be Pagiel the son of Ochran.

Num 2:28 His division, and those who were counted of them, were forty-one thousand and five hundred.

Num 2:29 "The tribe of Naphtali: and the prince of the children of Naphtali shall be Ahira the son of Enan.

Num 2:30 His division, and those who were counted of them, were fifty-three thousand four hundred.

MY NOTES

Num 2:31 "All who were counted of the camp of Dan were one hundred fifty-seven thousand six hundred. They shall set out last by their standards."

Num 2:32 These are those who were counted of the children of Israel by their fathers' houses. All who were counted of the camps according to their armies were six hundred three thousand five hundred fifty.

Num 2:33 But the Levites were not counted among the children of Israel; as YHWH commanded Moses.

Num 2:34 Thus the children of Israel did. According to all that YHWH commanded Moses, so they encamped by their standards, and so they set out, everyone by their families, according to their fathers' houses.

The Sons of Aaron

WEDNESDAY Num 3:1 Now this is the history of the generations of Aaron and Moses in the day that YHWH spoke with Moses in Mount Sinai.

Num 3:2 These are the names of the sons of Aaron: Nadab the firstborn, and Abihu, Eleazar, and Ithamar.

Num 3:3 These are the names of the sons of Aaron, the priests who were anointed, whom he consecrated to minister in the priest's office.

Num 3:4 Nadab and Abihu died before YHWH, when they offered strange fire before YHWH, in the wilderness of Sinai, and they had no children. Eleazar and Ithamar ministered in the priest's office in the presence of Aaron their father.

Duties of the Levites

Num 3:5 YHWH spoke to Moses, saying,

Num 3:6 "Bring the tribe of Levi near, and set them before Aaron the priest, that they may minister to him.

Num 3:7 They shall keep his requirements, and the requirements of the whole congregation before the Tent of Meeting, to do the service of the tabernacle.

Num 3:8 They shall keep all the furnishings of the Tent of Meeting, and the obligations of the children of Israel, to do the service of the tabernacle.

Num 3:9 You shall give the Levites to Aaron and to his sons. They are wholly given to him on the behalf of the children of Israel.

Num 3:10 You shall appoint Aaron and his sons, and they shall keep their priesthood. The stranger who comes near shall be put to death."

Num 3:11 YHWH spoke to Moses, saying,

MY NOTES

Num 3:12 *"Behold, I have taken the Levites from among the children of Israel instead of all the firstborn who open the womb among the children of Israel; and the Levites shall be mine:*

Num 3:13 for all the firstborn are mine. On the day that I struck down all the firstborn in the land of Egypt I made holy to me all the firstborn in Israel, both man and animal. They shall be mine. I am YHWH."

THURSDAY Num 3:14 YHWH spoke to Moses in the wilderness of Sinai, saying,

Num 3:15 "Count the children of Levi by their fathers' houses, by their families. You shall count every male from a month old and upward."

Num 3:16 Moses counted them according to YHWH's word, as he was commanded.

Num 3:17 These were the sons of Levi by their names: Gershon, and Kohath, and Merari.

Num 3:18 These are the names of the sons of Gershon by their families: Libni and Shimei.

Num 3:19 The sons of Kohath by their families: Amram, and Izhar, Hebron, and Uzziel.

Num 3:20 The sons of Merari by their families: Mahli and Mushi. These are the families of the Levites according to their fathers' houses.

Num 3:21 Of Gershon was the family of the Libnites, and the family of the Shimeites: these are the families of the Gershonites.

Num 3:22 Those who were counted of them, according to the number of all the males, from a month old and upward, even those who were counted of them were seven thousand five hundred.

Num 3:23 The families of the Gershonites shall encamp behind the tabernacle westward.

Num 3:24 The prince of the fathers' house of the Gershonites shall be Eliasaph the son of Lael.

Num 3:25 The duty of the sons of Gershon in the Tent of Meeting shall be the tabernacle, and the tent, its covering, and the screen for the door of the Tent of Meeting,

Num 3:26 and the hangings of the court, and the screen for the door of the court, which is by the tabernacle, and around the altar, and its cords for all of its service.

Num 3:27 Of Kohath was the family of the Amramites, and the family of the Izharites, and the family of the Hebronites, and the family of the Uzzielites: these are the families of the Kohathites.

MY NOTES

Num 3:28 According to the number of all the males, from a month old and upward, there were eight thousand six hundred, keeping the requirements of the sanctuary.

Num 3:29 The families of the sons of Kohath shall encamp on the south side of the tabernacle.

Num 3:30 The prince of the fathers' house of the families of the Kohathites shall be Elizaphan the son of Uzziel.

Num 3:31 Their duty shall be the ark, the table, the lamp stand, the altars, the vessels of the sanctuary with which they minister, and the screen, and all its service.

Num 3:32 Eleazar the son of Aaron the priest shall be prince of the princes of the Levites, with the oversight of those who keep the requirements of the sanctuary.

Num 3:33 Of Merari was the family of the Mahlites, and the family of the Mushites. These are the families of Merari.

Num 3:34 Those who were counted of them, according to the number of all the males, from a month old and upward, were six thousand two hundred.

Num 3:35 The prince of the fathers' house of the families of Merari was Zuriel the son of Abihail. They shall encamp on the north side of the tabernacle.

Num 3:36 The appointed duty of the sons of Merari shall be the tabernacle's boards, its bars, its pillars, its sockets, all its instruments, all its service,

Num 3:37 the pillars of the court around it, their sockets, their pins, and their cords.

Num 3:38 Those who encamp before the tabernacle eastward, in front of the Tent of Meeting toward the sunrise, shall be Moses, and Aaron and his sons, keeping the requirements of the sanctuary for the duty of the children of Israel. The stranger who comes near shall be put to death.

Num 3:39 **All who were counted of the Levites, whom Moses and Aaron counted at the commandment of YHWH, by their families, all the males from a month old and upward, were twenty-two thousand.**

Redemption of the Firstborn

FRIDAY Num 3:40 YHWH said to Moses, "Count all the firstborn males of the children of Israel from a month old and upward, and take the number of their names.

Num 3:41 You shall take the Levites for me (I am YHWH) instead of all the firstborn among the children of Israel; and the livestock of the Levites instead of all the firstborn among the livestock of the children of Israel."

Num 3:42 Moses counted, as YHWH commanded him, all the firstborn among the children of Israel.

Num 3:43 All the firstborn males according to the number of names, from a month old and upward, of those who were counted of them, were twenty-two thousand two hundred seventy-three.

Num 3:44 YHWH spoke to Moses, saying,

Num 3:45 "Take the Levites instead of all the firstborn among the children of Israel, and the livestock of the Levites instead of their livestock; and the Levites shall be mine. I am YHWH.

Num 3:46 *For the redemption of the two hundred seventy-three of the firstborn of the children of Israel, who exceed the number of the Levites,*

Num 3:47 you shall take five shekels apiece for each one; after the shekel of the sanctuary you shall take them (the shekel is twenty gerahs):

Num 3:48 and you shall give the money, with which their remainder is redeemed, to Aaron and to his sons."

Num 3:49 Moses took the redemption money from those who exceeded the number of those who were redeemed by the Levites;

Num 3:50 from the firstborn of the children of Israel he took the money, one thousand three hundred sixty-five shekels, after the shekel of the sanctuary:

Num 3:51 and Moses gave the redemption money to Aaron and to his sons, according to YHWH's word, as YHWH commanded Moses.

Duties of the Kohathites

SABBATH Num 4:1 YHWH spoke to Moses and to Aaron, saying,

Num 4:2 "Take a census of the sons of Kohath from among the sons of Levi, by their families, by their fathers' houses,

Num 4:3 from thirty years old and upward even until fifty years old, all who enter into the service, to do the work in the Tent of Meeting.

Num 4:4 "This is the service of the sons of Kohath in the Tent of Meeting, the most holy things.

Num 4:5 When the camp moves forward, Aaron shall go in, and his sons, and they shall take down the veil of the screen, and cover the ark of the Testimony with it,

Num 4:6 and shall put a covering of sealskin on it, and shall spread over it a cloth all of blue, and shall put in its poles.

Num 4:7 *"On the table of show bread they shall spread a blue cloth, and put on it the dishes, the spoons, the bowls, and the cups with which to pour out; and the continual bread shall be on it.*

MY NOTES

Num 4:8 They shall spread on them a scarlet cloth, and cover the same with a covering of sealskin, and shall put in its poles.

Num 4:9 "They shall take a blue cloth, and cover the lamp stand of the light, and its lamps, and its snuffers, and its snuff dishes, and all its oil vessels, with which they minister to it.

Num 4:10 They shall put it and all its vessels within a covering of sealskin, and shall put it on the frame.

Num 4:11 "On the golden altar they shall spread a blue cloth, and cover it with a covering of sealskin, and shall put in its poles.

Num 4:12 "They shall take all the vessels of ministry, with which they minister in the sanctuary, and put them in a blue cloth, and cover them with a covering of sealskin, and shall put them on the frame.

Num 4:13 "They shall take away the ashes from the altar, and spread a purple cloth on it.

Num 4:14 They shall put on it all its vessels, with which they minister about it, the fire pans, the meat hooks, the shovels, and the basins; all the vessels of the altar; and they shall spread on it a covering of sealskin, and put in its poles.

Num 4:15 "When Aaron and his sons have finished covering the sanctuary, and all the furniture of the sanctuary, as the camp moves forward; after that, the sons of Kohath shall come to carry it: but they shall not touch the sanctuary, lest they die. These things are the burden of the sons of Kohath in the Tent of Meeting.

Num 4:16 "The duty of Eleazar the son of Aaron the priest shall be the oil for the light, the sweet incense, the continual meal offering, and the anointing oil, the requirements of all the tabernacle, and of all that is in it, the sanctuary, and its furnishings."

Num 4:17 YHWH spoke to Moses and to Aaron, saying,

Num 4:18 "Don't cut off the tribe of the families of the Kohathites from among the Levites;

Num 4:19 but thus do to them, that they may live, and not die, when they approach the most holy things: Aaron and his sons shall go in, and appoint them everyone to his service and to his burden;

Num 4:20 but they shall not go in to see the sanctuary even for a moment, lest they die."

MY NOTES

BAMIDBAR WORDFIND

```
Y W S S M W C Y F U L P V O X E E V C R
O A G J S A I I F H I J U D A H U U Q P
E E F S E T O L S G S C G Q N A S O F E
K O H A T H I T E S K I E L E A Z A R D
J N G C I I E P H R A I M N Z Q Q Q F Z
Z E O X N N V E A Q N F R E S O I R E E
I L K C O L R G Q N K E G N O U M R G B
Z C B B H M Z E B N I O S Q N N S E E U
J A A Q S C F H U E D M X S C I X H M L
O N X W R U X U W B D Q A L K P J S B U
F R M J E G B B Y M E S J J M F T A G N
A E Q F G W M G B C N N I J N K O E B P
H B N Y T A B G M V A V D A G E H C B M
E A A J F L Y N E C P F I D A R B Y X H
S T W S X J V K L W H E P E H X O N O N
S C A B M E R A R I T E S H S O N D I U
A W K P L C R A H C A S S I T V Z A G L
N O K Z U J U D I F L R A F A K X D J M
A T Q S F V Q A P V I A G T R I B E S P
M P A Z B O L N Z C I M V M F R O B D K
```

REUBEN	SIMEON	JUDAH	ISSACHAR
ZEBULUN	EPHRAIM	MANASSEH	BENJAMIN
DAN	ASHER	GAD	NAPHTALI
MERARITES	GERSHONITES	KOHATHITES	WILERNESS
ELEAZAR	CENSUS	TABERNACLE	TRIBES

CRYPTOGRAM – HOSEA 1:10

A	B	C	D	E	F	G	H	I	J	K	L	M	N	O	P	Q	R	S	T	U	V	W	X	Y	Z
2			16					4			24		22												

VERSE FIND – LUKE 16:10

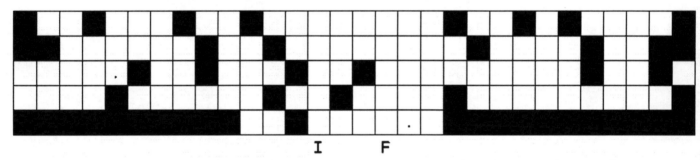

```
            I       F
  R     I     SE    MUTHSO    N  A      EN
  U LI   HOE   IHFFITCLFU   OILHT    IS
V ECYTLHTTLSOAASAHUSHDNESONINT
MHEHWTLEIWINISIHDILLIASSOVERYA
```

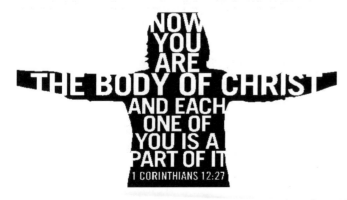

READ 1 Corinthians 12:12-31

page 20

NASO

נָשֹׂא

NUMBERS

It Means: ELEVATE!

Our Thirty-fifth Torah Portion is called Naso! נָשֹׂא
Numbers 4:21 – Numbers 7:89
PROPHETS: Judges 13:2-25
NEW TESTAMENT: Matthew 26:14-45; 27:34; John 7:37-8:11; Acts 21:17-32

MAKE A MARK

Each time you hear someone say one of the words below make a '✓" beside the word. See how many marks you can get!

census	
tabernacle	
husband	
jealous	
Levites	
offering	

FIRST FIND

~

If someone mentions a verse or scripture that is NOT in this Torah Portion, see if YOU can be the First to Find it!

This Weeks Torah Portion is:

Parsha: _____

Scriptures: _____

Name: _____

words I didn't Understand

?!

My Favorite Song was:

date:

I talked to _____
about Today's Study.

The Most IMPORTANT
thing I Learned today was:

MY NOTES

Draw something you learned today

I brought My Bible with me ☐
✔ I am sitting with my Family ☐
I am ready to listen Carefully ☐

May YHWH bless you, and keep you. YHWH make his face to shine on you and be gracious to you. YHWH lift up his face toward you, and give you peace.

SUNDAY Num 4:21 YHWH spoke to Moses, saying,

Num 4:22 "Take a census of the sons of Gershon also, by their fathers' houses, by their families;

Num 4:23 you shall count them from thirty years old and upward until fifty years old; all who enter in to wait on the service, to do the work in the Tent of Meeting.

Num 4:24 "This is the service of the families of the Gershonites, in serving and in bearing burdens:

Num 4:25 they shall carry the curtains of the tabernacle, and the Tent of Meeting, its covering, and the covering of sealskin that is above on it, and the screen for the door of the Tent of Meeting,

Num 4:26 and the hangings of the court, and the screen for the door of the gate of the court, which is by the tabernacle and around the altar, and their cords, and all the instruments of their service, and whatever shall be done with them. They shall serve in there.

Num 4:27 *At the commandment of Aaron and his sons shall be all the service of the sons of the Gershonites, in all their burden, and in all their service; and you shall appoint their duty to them in all their responsibilities.*

Num 4:28 This is the service of the families of the sons of the Gershonites in the Tent of Meeting: and their duty shall be under the hand of Ithamar the son of Aaron the priest.

Num 4:29 "As for the sons of Merari, you shall count them by their families, by their fathers' houses;

Num 4:30 you shall count them from thirty years old and upward even to fifty years old, everyone who enters on the service, to do the work of the Tent of Meeting.

Num 4:31 This is the duty of their burden, according to all their service in the Tent of Meeting: the tabernacle's boards, its bars, its pillars, its sockets,

Num 4:32 and the pillars of the court around it, and their sockets, and their pins, and their cords, with all their instruments, and with all their service: and by name you shall appoint the instruments of the duty of their burden.

Num 4:33 This is the service of the families of the sons of Merari, according to all their service, in the Tent of Meeting, under the hand of Ithamar the son of Aaron the priest."

Num 4:34 Moses and Aaron and the princes of the congregation counted the sons of the Kohathites by their families, and by their fathers' houses,

Num 4:35 from thirty years old and upward even to fifty years old, everyone who entered into the service, for work in the Tent of Meeting.

Num 4:36 Those who were counted of them by their families were two thousand seven hundred fifty.

MY NOTES

Num 4:36 Those who were counted of them by their families were two thousand seven hundred fifty.

Num 4:37 These are those who were counted of the families of the Kohathites, all who served in the Tent of Meeting, whom Moses and Aaron counted according to the commandment of YHWH by Moses.

MONDAY Num 4:38 Those who were counted of the sons of Gershon, their families, and by their fathers' houses,

Num 4:39 from thirty years old and upward even to fifty years old, everyone who entered into the service, for work in the Tent of Meeting,

Num 4:40 even those who were counted of them, by their families, by their fathers' houses, were two thousand six hundred thirty.

Num 4:41 These are those who were counted of the families of the sons of Gershon, all who served in the Tent of Meeting, whom Moses and Aaron counted according to the commandment of YHWH.

Num 4:42 Those who were counted of the families of the sons of Merari, by their families, by their fathers' houses,

Num 4:43 from thirty years old and upward even to fifty years old, everyone who entered into the service, for work in the Tent of Meeting,

Num 4:44 even those who were counted of them by their families, were three thousand two hundred.

Num 4:45 These are those who were counted of the families of the sons of Merari, whom Moses and Aaron counted according to the commandment of YHWH by Moses.

Num 4:46 All those who were counted of the Levites, whom Moses and Aaron and the princes of Israel counted, by their families, and by their fathers' houses,

Num 4:47 from thirty years old and upward even to fifty years old, everyone who entered in to do the work of service, and the work of bearing burdens in the Tent of Meeting,

Num 4:48 even those who were counted of them, were eight thousand five hundred eighty.

Num 4:49 *According to the commandment of YHWH they were counted by Moses, everyone according to his service, and according to his burden. Thus were they counted by him, as YHWH commanded Moses.*

MY NOTES

Unclean People

TUESDAY Num 5:1 YHWH spoke to Moses, saying,

Num 5:2 "Command the children of Israel that they put out of the camp every leper, and everyone who has an issue, and whoever is unclean by the dead.

Num 5:3 Both you shall put male and female outside of the camp; that they not defile their camp, in the midst of which I dwell."

Num 5:4 The children of Israel did so, and put them outside of the camp; as YHWH spoke to Moses, so did the children of Israel.

Confession and Restitution

Num 5:5 YHWH spoke to Moses, saying,

Num 5:6 *"Speak to the children of Israel: 'When a man or woman commits any sin that men commit, so as to trespass against YHWH, and that soul is guilty;*

Num 5:7 then he shall confess his sin which he has done, and he shall make restitution for his guilt in full, and add to it the fifth part of it, and give it to him in respect of whom he has been guilty.

Num 5:8 But if the man has no kinsman to whom restitution may be made for the guilt, the restitution for guilt which is made to YHWH shall be the priest's; in addition to the ram of the atonement, by which atonement shall be made for him.

Num 5:9 Every heave offering of all the holy things of the children of Israel, which they present to the priest, shall be his.

Num 5:10 Every man's holy things shall be his: whatever any man gives the priest, it shall be his.'"

A Test for Adultery

WEDNESDAY Num 5:11 YHWH spoke to Moses, saying,

Num 5:12 "Speak to the children of Israel, and tell them: 'If any man's wife goes astray, and is unfaithful to him,

Num 5:13 and a man lies with her carnally, and it is hidden from the eyes of her husband, and this is kept concealed, and she is defiled, and there is no witness against her, and she isn't taken in the act;

Num 5:14 and the spirit of jealousy comes on him, and he is jealous of his wife, and she is defiled: or if the spirit of jealousy comes on him, and he is jealous of his wife, and she isn't defiled:

Num 5:15 then the man shall bring his wife to the priest, and shall bring her offering for her: one tenth of an ephah of barley meal. He shall pour no oil on it, nor put frankincense on it, for it is a meal offering of jealousy, a meal offering of memorial, bringing iniquity to memory.

MY NOTES

Num 5:16 The priest shall bring her near, and set her before YHWH;

Num 5:17 and the priest shall take holy water in an earthen vessel; and of the dust that is on the floor of the tabernacle the priest shall take, and put it into the water.

Num 5:18 The priest shall set the woman before YHWH, and let the hair of the woman's head go loose, and put the meal offering of memorial in her hands, which is the meal offering of jealousy. The priest shall have in his hand the water of bitterness that brings a curse.

Num 5:19 The priest shall cause her to swear, and shall tell the woman, "If no man has lain with you, and if you haven't gone aside to uncleanness, being under your husband, be free from this water of bitterness that brings a curse.

Num 5:20 But if you have gone astray, being under your husband, and if you are defiled, and some man has lain with you besides your husband:"

Num 5:21 then the priest shall cause the woman to swear with the oath of cursing, and the priest shall tell the woman, "YHWH make you a curse and an oath among your people, when YHWH allows your thigh to fall away, and your body to swell;

Num 5:22 and this water that brings a curse will go into your bowels, and make your body swell, and your thigh fall away." The woman shall say, "Amen, Amen."

Num 5:23 **"'The priest shall write these curses in a book, and he shall blot them out into the water of bitterness.**

Num 5:24 He shall make the woman drink the water of bitterness that causes the curse; and the water that causes the curse shall enter into her and become bitter.

Num 5:25 The priest shall take the meal offering of jealousy out of the woman's hand, and shall wave the meal offering before YHWH, and bring it to the altar.

Num 5:26 The priest shall take a handful of the meal offering, as its memorial, and burn it on the altar, and afterward shall make the woman drink the water.

Num 5:27 When he has made her drink the water, then it shall happen, if she is defiled, and has committed a trespass against her husband, that the water that causes the curse will enter into her and become bitter, and her body will swell, and her thigh will fall away: and the woman will be a curse among her people.

Num 5:28 If the woman isn't defiled, but is clean; then she shall be free, and shall conceive offspring.

Num 5:29 "'This is the law of jealousy, when a wife, being under her husband, goes astray, and is defiled;

MY NOTES

Num 5:30 or when the spirit of jealousy comes on a man, and he is jealous of his wife; then he shall set the woman before YHWH, and the priest shall execute on her all this law.

Num 5:31 The man shall be free from iniquity, and that woman shall bear her iniquity.'"

The Nazirite Vow

Num 6:1 YHWH spoke to Moses, saying,

Num 6:2 "Speak to the children of Israel, and tell them: 'When either man or woman shall make a special vow, the vow of a Nazirite, to separate himself to YHWH,

Num 6:3 he shall separate himself from wine and strong drink. He shall drink no vinegar of wine, or vinegar of fermented drink, neither shall he drink any juice of grapes, nor eat fresh grapes or dried.

Num 6:4 All the days of his separation he shall eat nothing that is made of the grapevine, from the seeds even to the skins.

Num 6:5 "'All the days of his vow of separation no razor shall come on his head, until the days are fulfilled, in which he separates himself to YHWH. He shall be holy. He shall let the locks of the hair of his head grow long.

Num 6:6 "'All the days that he separates himself to YHWH he shall not go near a dead body.

Num 6:7 He shall not make himself unclean for his father, or for his mother, for his brother, or for his sister, when they die; because his separation to God is on his head.

Num 6:8 All the days of his separation he is holy to YHWH.

Num 6:9 "'If any man dies very suddenly beside him, and he defiles the head of his separation; then he shall shave his head in the day of his cleansing. On the seventh day he shall shave it.

Num 6:10 On the eighth day he shall bring two turtledoves or two young pigeons to the priest, to the door of the Tent of Meeting.

Num 6:11 The priest shall offer one for a sin offering, and the other for a burnt offering, and make atonement for him, because he sinned by reason of the dead, and shall make his head holy that same day.

Num 6:12 He shall separate to YHWH the days of his separation, and shall bring a male lamb a year old for a trespass offering; but the former days shall be void, because his separation was defiled.

Num 6:13 "'This is the law of the Nazirite: when the days of his separation are fulfilled, he shall be brought to the door of the Tent of Meeting,

MY NOTES

Num 6:14 and he shall offer his offering to YHWH, one male lamb a year old without defect for a burnt offering, and one ewe lamb a year old without defect for a sin offering, and one ram without defect for peace offerings,

Num 6:15 and a basket of unleavened bread, cakes of fine flour mixed with oil, and unleavened wafers anointed with oil, and their meal offering, and their drink offerings.

Num 6:16 The priest shall present them before YHWH, and shall offer his sin offering, and his burnt offering.

Num 6:17 He shall offer the ram for a sacrifice of peace offerings to YHWH, with the basket of unleavened bread. The priest shall offer also its meal offering, and its drink offering.

Num 6:18 The Nazirite shall shave the head of his separation at the door of the Tent of Meeting, and shall take the hair of the head of his separation, and put it on the fire which is under the sacrifice of peace offerings.

Num 6:19 The priest shall take the boiled shoulder of the ram, and one unleavened cake out of the basket, and one unleavened wafer, and shall put them on the hands of the Nazirite, after he has shaved the head of his separation;

Num 6:20 and the priest shall wave them for a wave offering before YHWH. This is holy for the priest, together with the breast that is waved and the thigh that is offered. After that the Nazirite may drink wine.

Num 6:21 "'This is the law of the Nazirite who vows, and of his offering to YHWH for his separation, in addition to that which he is able to get. According to his vow which he vows, so he must do after the law of his separation.'"

Aaron's Blessing

Num 6:22 YHWH spoke to Moses, saying,

Num 6:23 "Speak to Aaron and to his sons, saying, 'This is how you shall bless the children of Israel.' You shall tell them,

Num 6:24 'YHWH bless you, and keep you.

Num 6:25 YHWH make his face to shine on you, and be gracious to you.

Num 6:26 YHWH lift up his face toward you, and give you peace.'

Num 6:27 "So they shall put my name on the children of Israel; and I will bless them."

Offerings at the Tabernacle's Consecration

THURSDAY Num 7:1 On the day that Moses had finished setting up the tabernacle, and had anointed it and sanctified it, with all its furniture, and the altar with all its vessels, and had anointed and sanctified them;

MY NOTES

Num 7:2 the princes of Israel, the heads of their fathers' houses, offered. These were the princes of the tribes. These are they who were over those who were counted:

Num 7:3 and they brought their offering before YHWH, six covered wagons, and twelve oxen; a wagon for every two of the princes, and for each one an ox: and they presented them before the tabernacle.

Num 7:4 YHWH spoke to Moses, saying,

Num 7:5 "Accept these from them, that they may be used in doing the service of the Tent of Meeting; and you shall give them to the Levites, to every man according to his service."

Num 7:6 Moses took the wagons and the oxen, and gave them to the Levites.

Num 7:7 He gave two wagons and four oxen to the sons of Gershon, according to their service:

Num 7:8 and he gave four wagons and eight oxen to the sons of Merari, according to their service, under the direction of Ithamar the son of Aaron the priest.

Num 7:9 But to the sons of Kohath he gave none, because the service of the sanctuary belonged to them; they carried it on their shoulders.

Num 7:10 **The princes gave offerings for the dedication of the altar in the day that it was anointed, even the princes gave their offerings before the altar.**

Num 7:11 YHWH said to Moses, "They shall offer their offering, each prince on his day, for the dedication of the altar."

Num 7:12 He who offered his offering the first day was Nahshon the son of Amminadab, of the tribe of Judah,

Num 7:13 and his offering was: one silver platter, the weight of which was one hundred thirty shekels,one silver bowl of seventy shekels, after the shekel of the sanctuary; both of them full of fine flour mixed with oil for a meal offering;

Num 7:14 one golden ladle of ten shekels, full of incense;

Num 7:15 one young bull, one ram, one male lamb a year old, for a burnt offering;

Num 7:16 one male goat for a sin offering;

Num 7:17 and for the sacrifice of peace offerings, two head of cattle, five rams, five male goats, and five male lambs a year old. This was the offering of Nahshon the son of Amminadab.

Num 7:18 On the second day Nethanel the son of Zuar, prince of Issachar, gave his offering.

Num 7:19 He offered for his offering: one silver platter, the weight of which was one hundred thirty shekels, one silver bowl of seventy shekels, after the shekel of the sanctuary; both of them full of fine flour mixed with oil for a meal offering;

MY NOTES

Num 7:20 one golden ladle of ten shekels, full of incense;

Num 7:21 one young bull, one ram, one male lamb a year old, for a burnt offering;

Num 7:22 one male goat for a sin offering;

Num 7:23 and for the sacrifice of peace offerings, two head of cattle, five rams, five male goats, five male lambs a year old. This was the offering of Nethanel the son of Zuar.

Num 7:24 On the third day Eliab the son of Helon, prince of the children of Zebulun

Num 7:25 gave his offering: one silver platter, the weight of which was a hundred and thirty shekels, one silver bowl of seventy shekels, after the shekel of the sanctuary; both of them full of fine flour mixed with oil for a meal offering;

Num 7:26 one golden ladle of ten shekels, full of incense;

Num 7:27 one young bull, one ram, one male lamb a year old, for a burnt offering;

Num 7:28 one male goat for a sin offering;

Num 7:29 and for the sacrifice of peace offerings, two head of cattle, five rams, five male goats, and five male lambs a year old. This was the offering of Eliab the son of Helon.

Num 7:30 On the fourth day Elizur the son of Shedeur, prince of the children of Reuben

Num 7:31 gave his offering: one silver platter, the weight of which was one hundred thirty shekels, one silver bowl of seventy shekels, after the shekel of the sanctuary; both of them full of fine flour mixed with oil for a meal offering;

Num 7:32 one golden ladle of ten shekels, full of incense;

Num 7:33 one young bull, one ram, one male lamb a year old, for a burnt offering;

Num 7:34 one male goat for a sin offering;

Num 7:35 and for the sacrifice of peace offerings, two head of cattle, five rams, five male goats, and five male lambs a year old. This was the offering of Elizur the son of Shedeur.

Num 7:36 On the fifth day Shelumiel the son of Zurishaddai, prince of the children of Simeon

Num 7:37 gave his offering: one silver platter, the weight of which was one hundred thirty shekels, one silver bowl of seventy shekels, after the shekel of the sanctuary; both of them full of fine flour mixed with oil for a meal offering;

Num 7:38 one golden ladle of ten shekels, full of incense;

Num 7:39 one young bull, one ram, one male lamb a year old, for a burnt offering;

Num 7:40 one male goat for a sin offering;

MY NOTES

Num 7:41 and for the sacrifice of peace offerings, two head of cattle, five rams, five male goats, and five male lambs a year old: this was the offering of Shelumiel the son of Zurishaddai.

FRIDAY Num 7:42 On the sixth day, Eliasaph the son of Deuel, prince of the children of Gad

Num 7:43 gave his offering: one silver platter, the weight of which was one hundred thirty shekels, one silver bowl of seventy shekels, after the shekel of the sanctuary; both of them full of fine flour mixed with oil for a meal offering;

Num 7:44 one golden ladle of ten shekels, full of incense;

Num 7:45 one young bull, one ram, one male lamb a year old, for a burnt offering;

Num 7:46 *one male goat for a sin offering;*

Num 7:47 and for the sacrifice of peace offerings, two head of cattle, five rams, five male goats, and five male lambs a year old. This was the offering of Eliasaph the son of Deuel.

Num 7:48 On the seventh day Elishama the son of Ammihud, prince of the children of Ephraim

Num 7:49 gave his offering: one silver platter, the weight of which was one hundred thirty shekels, one silver bowl of seventy shekels, after the shekel of the sanctuary; both of them full of fine flour mixed with oil for a meal offering;

Num 7:50 one golden ladle of ten shekels, full of incense;

Num 7:51 one young bull, one ram, one male lamb a year old, for a burnt offering;

Num 7:52 *one male goat for a sin offering;*

Num 7:53 and for the sacrifice of peace offerings, two head of cattle, five rams, five male goats, and five male lambs a year old. This was the offering of Elishama the son of Ammihud.

Num 7:54 On the eighth day Gamaliel the son of Pedahzur, prince of the children of Manasseh

Num 7:55 gave his offering: one silver platter, the weight of which was one hundred thirty shekels, one silver bowl of seventy shekels, after the shekel of the sanctuary; both of them full of fine flour mixed with oil for a meal offering;

Num 7:56 one golden ladle of ten shekels, full of incense;

Num 7:57 one young bull, one ram, one male lamb a year old, for a burnt offering;

Num 7:58 *one male goat for a sin offering;*

Num 7:59 and for the sacrifice of peace offerings, two head of cattle, five rams, five male goats, and five male lambs a year old. This was the offering of Gamaliel the son of Pedahzur.

Num 7:60 On the ninth day Abidan the son of Gideoni, prince of the children of Benjamin

MY NOTES

Num 7:61 gave his offering: one silver platter, the weight of which was one hundred thirty shekels, one silver bowl of seventy shekels, after the shekel of the sanctuary; both of them full of fine flour mixed with oil for a meal offering;

Num 7:62 one golden ladle of ten shekels, full of incense;

Num 7:63 one young bull, one ram, one male lamb a year old, for a burnt offering;

Num 7:64 one male goat for a sin offering;

Num 7:65 and for the sacrifice of peace offerings, two head of cattle, five rams, five male goats, and five male lambs a year old. This was the offering of Abidan the son of Gideoni.

Num 7:66 On the tenth day Ahiezer the son of Ammishaddai, prince of the children of Dan

Num 7:67 gave his offering: one silver platter, the weight of which was one hundred thirty shekels, one silver bowl of seventy shekels, after the shekel of the sanctuary; both of them full of fine flour mixed with oil for a meal offering;

Num 7:68 one golden ladle of ten shekels, full of incense;

Num 7:69 one young bull, one ram, one male lamb a year old, for a burnt offering;

Num 7:70 one male goat for a sin offering;

Num 7:71 and for the sacrifice of peace offerings, two head of cattle, five rams, five male goats, and five male lambs a year old. This was the offering of Ahiezer the son of Ammishaddai.

SABBATH Num 7:72 On the eleventh day Pagiel the son of Ochran, prince of the children of Asher

Num 7:73 gave his offering: one silver platter, the weight of which was one hundred thirty shekels, one silver bowl of seventy shekels, after the shekel of the sanctuary; both of them full of fine flour mixed with oil for a meal offering;

Num 7:74 one golden ladle of ten shekels, full of incense;

Num 7:75 one young bull, one ram, one male lamb a year old, for a burnt offering;

Num 7:76 one male goat for a sin offering;

Num 7:77 and for the sacrifice of peace offerings, two head of cattle, five rams, five male goats, and five male lambs a year old. This was the offering of Pagiel the son of Ochran.

Num 7:78 On the twelfth day Ahira the son of Enan, prince of the children of Naphtali

Num 7:79 gave his offering: one silver platter, the weight of which was one hundred thirty shekels, one silver bowl of seventy shekels, after the shekel of the sanctuary; both of them full of fine flour mixed with oil for a meal offering;

MY NOTES

Num 7:80 one golden spoon of ten shekels, full of incense;

Num 7:81 one young bull, one ram, one male lamb a year old, for a burnt offering;

Num 7:82 one male goat for a sin offering;

Num 7:83 and for the sacrifice of peace offerings, two head of cattle, five rams, five male goats, and five male lambs a year old. This was the offering of Ahira the son of Enan.

Num 7:84 This was the dedication of the altar, on the day when it was anointed, by the princes of Israel: twelve silver platters, twelve silver bowls, twelve golden ladles;

Num 7:85 each silver platter weighing one hundred thirty shekels, and each bowl seventy; all the silver of the vessels two thousand four hundred shekels, after the shekel of the sanctuary;

Num 7:86 the twelve golden ladles, full of incense, weighing ten shekels apiece, after the shekel of the sanctuary; all the gold of the ladles weighed one hundred twenty shekels;

Num 7:87 all the cattle for the burnt offering twelve bulls, the rams twelve, the male lambs a year old twelve, and their meal offering; and the male goats for a sin offering twelve;

Num 7:88 and all the cattle for the sacrifice of peace offerings twenty-four bulls, the rams sixty, the male goats sixty, the male lambs a year old sixty. This was the dedication of the altar, after it was anointed.

Num 7:89 ***When Moses went into the Tent of Meeting to speak with YHWH, he heard his voice speaking to him from above the mercy seat that was on the ark of the Testimony, from between the two cherubim: and he spoke to him.***

Yeshua in the Old Testament

John 1:14 (NKJV)

And the Word became flesh and dwelt (tabernacled) among us...

Revelation 21:3 (NKJV)

3 And I heard a loud voice from heaven saying, "Behold, the **tabernacle** of God *is* with men, and He will dwell with them, and they shall be His people. God Himself will be with them *and be* their God.

NASO SCRAMBLE

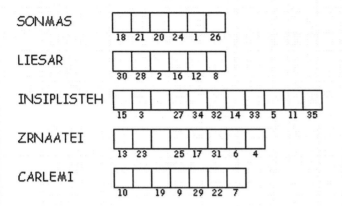

SONMAS
18 21 20 24 1 26

LIESAR
30 28 2 16 12 8

INSIPLISTEH
15 3 ___ 27 34 32 14 33 5 11 35

ZRNAATEI
13 23 ___ 25 17 31 6 4

CARLEMI
10 ___ 19 9 29 22 7

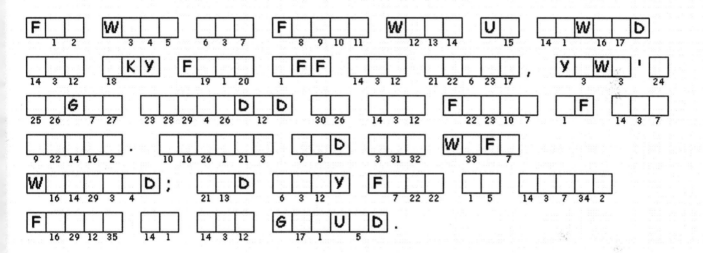

F _ _ W _ _ _ _ _ _ F _ _ _ _ W _ _ _ U _ _ W _ D
1 2 3 4 5 6 7 8 9 10 11 12 13 14 15 14 1 16 17

_ _ _ K Y F _ _ _ F F _ _ _ _ _ _ _ , Y W _ '
14 3 12 18 19 1 20 1 14 3 12 21 22 6 23 17 3 3 24

_ _ G _ _ _ _ _ _ D _ D _ _ _ _ _ _ F _ _ _ _ F _ _
25 26 7 27 23 28 29 4 26 12 30 26 14 3 12 22 23 10 7 1 14 3 7

_ _ _ _ _ . _ _ _ _ _ _ _ D _ _ W _ F _
9 22 14 16 2 10 16 26 1 21 3 9 5 3 31 32 33 7

W _ _ _ _ D ; _ _ D _ _ _ Y F _ _ _ _ _ _ _ _
16 14 29 3 4 21 13 6 3 12 7 22 22 1 5 14 3 7 34 2

F _ _ _ _ _ _ _ _ G _ U _ D .
16 29 12 35 14 1 14 3 12 17 1 5

VERSE FIND – ACTS 21:19

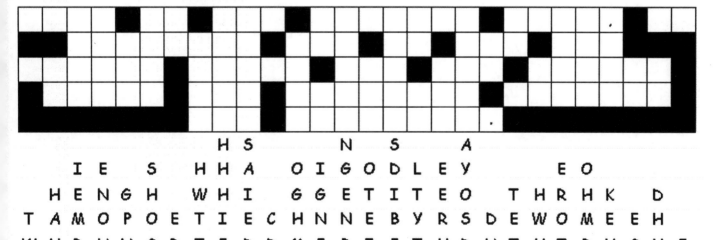

BEHAALOTECHA

בְּהַעֲלֹתְךָ

NUMBERS

It Means: WHEN YOU STEP UP!

Our Thirty-Sixth Torah Portion is called Beha'alo-techa!

בְּהַעֲלֹתְךָ

Numbers 8:1 – Numbers 12:16

PROPHETS: Zechariah 2:1 - 4:7

NEW TESTAMENT: Luke 17:11–18:14; 23:44-56; Acts 2; 10; 2 Corinthians 10:5-13; Hebrews 3:1-6; Revelation 11:1-3

MAKE A MARK

Each time you hear someone say one of the words below make a '/" beside the word. See how many marks you can get!

lamps	
fifty	
Passover	
cloud	
fire	
quail	

FIRST FIND

~

If someone mentions a verse or scripture that is NOT in this Torah Portion, see if YOU can be the First to Find it!

This Weeks Torah Portion is:

Parsha: _____

Scriptures: _____

Name: _____

My Favorite Song was:

date:

I talked to _____
about Today's Study.

words I didn't Understand

The Most IMPORTANT
thing I Learned today was:

MY NOTES

Draw something you learned today

I brought My Bible with me ☐
☑ I am sitting with my Family ☐
I am ready to listen Carefully ☐

The Seven Lamps

SUNDAY Num 8:1 YHWH spoke to Moses, saying,

Num 8:2 *"Speak to Aaron, and tell him, 'When you light the lamps, the seven lamps shall give light in front of the lamp stand.'"*

Num 8:3 Aaron did so. He lit its lamps to light the area in front of the lamp stand, as YHWH commanded Moses.

Num 8:4 This was the workmanship of the lamp stand, beaten work of gold. From its base to its flowers, it was beaten work: according to the pattern which YHWH had shown Moses, so he made the lamp stand.

Cleansing of the Levites

Num 8:5 YHWH spoke to Moses, saying,

Num 8:6 "Take the Levites from among the children of Israel, and cleanse them.

Num 8:7 You shall do this to them, to cleanse them: sprinkle the water of cleansing on them, let them shave their whole bodies with a razor, and let them wash their clothes, and cleanse themselves.

Num 8:8 Then let them take a young bull, and its meal offering, fine flour mixed with oil; and another young bull you shall take for a sin offering.

Num 8:9 You shall present the Levites before the Tent of Meeting. You shall assemble the whole congregation of the children of Israel.

Num 8:10 You shall present the Levites before YHWH. The children of Israel shall lay their hands on the Levites,

Num 8:11 and Aaron shall offer the Levites before YHWH for a wave offering, on the behalf of the children of Israel, that it may be theirs to do the service of YHWH.

Num 8:12 "The Levites shall lay their hands on the heads of the bulls, and you shall offer the one for a sin offering, and the other for a burnt offering to YHWH, to make atonement for the Levites.

Num 8:13 You shall set the Levites before Aaron, and before his sons, and offer them as a wave offering to YHWH.

Num 8:14 Thus you shall separate the Levites from among the children of Israel, and the Levites shall be mine.

MONDAY Num 8:15 "After that, the Levites shall go in to do the service of the Tent of Meeting: and you shall cleanse them, and offer them as a wave offering.

Num 8:16 For they are wholly given to me from among the children of Israel; instead of all who open the womb, even the firstborn of all the children of Israel, I have taken them to me.

MY NOTES

Num 8:17 For all the firstborn among the children of Israel are mine, both man and animal. On the day that I struck all the firstborn in the land of Egypt, I sanctified them for myself.

Num 8:18 I have taken the Levites instead of all the firstborn among the children of Israel.

Num 8:19 *I have given the Levites as a gift to Aaron and to his sons from among the children of Israel, to do the service of the children of Israel in the Tent of Meeting, and to make atonement for the children of Israel; that there be no plague among the children of Israel, when the children of Israel come near to the sanctuary."*

Num 8:20 Moses, and Aaron, and all the congregation of the children of Israel did so to the Levites. According to all that YHWH commanded Moses concerning the Levites, so the children of Israel did to them.

Num 8:21 The Levites purified themselves from sin, and they washed their clothes; and Aaron offered them for a wave offering before YHWH; and Aaron made atonement for them to cleanse them.

Num 8:22 After that, the Levites went in to do their service in the Tent of Meeting before Aaron, and before his sons: as YHWH had commanded Moses concerning the Levites, so they did to them.

Retirement of the Levites

Num 8:23 YHWH spoke to Moses, saying,

Num 8:24 "This is that which belongs to the Levites: from twenty-five years old and upward they shall go in to wait on the service in the work of the Tent of Meeting;

Num 8:25 and from the age of fifty years they shall cease waiting on the work, and shall serve no more,

Num 8:26 but shall minister with their brothers in the Tent of Meeting, to perform the duty, and shall perform no service. You shall do thus to the Levites concerning their duties."

The Passover Celebrated

TUESDAY Num 9:1 YHWH spoke to Moses in the wilderness of Sinai, in the first month of the second year after they had come out of the land of Egypt, saying,

Num 9:2 *"Moreover let the children of Israel keep the Passover in its appointed season.*

Num 9:3 On the fourteenth day of this month, at evening, you shall keep it in its appointed season—according to all its statutes, and according to all its ordinances, you shall keep it."

Num 9:4 Moses spoke to the children of Israel, that they should keep the Passover.

Num 9:5 ***They kept the Passover in the first month, on the fourteenth day of the month, at evening, in the wilderness of Sinai. According to all that YHWH commanded Moses, so the children of Israel did.***

Num 9:6 There were certain men, who were unclean because of the dead body of a man, so that they could not keep the Passover on that day, and they came before Moses and before Aaron on that day.

Num 9:7 Those men said to him, "We are unclean because of the dead body of a man. Why are we kept back, that we may not offer the offering of YHWH in its appointed season among the children of Israel?"

Num 9:8 Moses answered them, "Wait, that I may hear what YHWH will command concerning you."

Num 9:9 YHWH spoke to Moses, saying,

Num 9:10 "Say to the children of Israel, 'If any man of you or of your generations is unclean by reason of a dead body, or is on a journey far away, he shall still keep the Passover to YHWH.

Num 9:11 In the second month, on the fourteenth day at evening they shall keep it; they shall eat it with unleavened bread and bitter herbs.

Num 9:12 They shall leave none of it until the morning, nor break a bone of it. According to all the statute of the Passover they shall keep it.

Num 9:13 But the man who is clean, and is not on a journey, and fails to keep the Passover, that soul shall be cut off from his people. Because he didn't offer the offering of YHWH in its appointed season, that man shall bear his sin.

Num 9:14 ***"'If a foreigner lives among you, and desires to keep the Passover to YHWH; according to the statute of the Passover, and according to its ordinance, so shall he do. You shall have one statute, both for the foreigner, and for him who is born in the land.'"***

The Cloud Covering the Tabernacle

<u>WEDNESDAY</u> Num 9:15 On the day that the tabernacle was raised up, the cloud covered the tabernacle, even the Tent of the Testimony: and at evening it was over the tabernacle, as it were the appearance of fire, until morning.

Num 9:16 So it was continually. The cloud covered it, and the appearance of fire by night.

Num 9:17 Whenever the cloud was taken up from over the Tent, then after that the children of Israel traveled; and in the place where the cloud remained, there the children of Israel encamped.

MY NOTES

Num 9:18 At the commandment of YHWH, the children of Israel traveled, and at the commandment of YHWH they encamped. As long as the cloud remained on the tabernacle they remained encamped.

Num 9:19 When the cloud stayed on the tabernacle many days, then the children of Israel kept YHWH's command, and didn't travel.

Num 9:20 Sometimes the cloud was a few days on the tabernacle; then according to the commandment of YHWH they remained encamped, and according to the commandment of YHWH they traveled.

Num 9:21 *Sometimes the cloud was from evening until morning; and when the cloud was taken up in the morning, they traveled: or by day and by night, when the cloud was taken up, they traveled.*

Num 9:22 Whether it was two days, or a month, or a year that the cloud stayed on the tabernacle, remaining on it, the children of Israel remained encamped, and didn't travel; but when it was taken up, they traveled.

Num 9:23 At the commandment of YHWH they encamped, and at the commandment of YHWH they traveled. They kept YHWH's command, at the commandment of YHWH by Moses.

The Silver Trumpets

Num 10:1 YHWH spoke to Moses, saying,

Num 10:2 "Make two trumpets of silver. You shall make them of beaten work. You shall use them for the calling of the congregation, and for the journeying of the camps.

Num 10:3 When they blow them, all the congregation shall gather themselves to you at the door of the Tent of Meeting.

Num 10:4 If they blow just one, then the princes, the heads of the thousands of Israel, shall gather themselves to you.

Num 10:5 When you blow an alarm, the camps that lie on the east side shall go forward.

Num 10:6 When you blow an alarm the second time, the camps that lie on the south side shall go forward. They shall blow an alarm for their journeys.

Num 10:7 But when the assembly is to be gathered together, you shall blow, but you shall not sound an alarm.

Num 10:8 "The sons of Aaron, the priests, shall blow the trumpets. This shall be to you for a statute forever throughout your generations.

Num 10:9 When you go to war in your land against the adversary who oppresses you, then you shall sound an alarm with the trumpets. Then you will be remembered before YHWH your God, and you will be saved from your enemies.

MY NOTES

Num 10:10 "Also in the day of your gladness, and in your set feasts, and in the beginnings of your months, you shall blow the trumpets over your burnt offerings, and over the sacrifices of your peace offerings; and they shall be to you for a memorial before your God. I am YHWH your God."

Israel Leaves Sinai

THURSDAY Num 10:11 *In the second year, in the second month, on the twentieth day of the month, the cloud was taken up from over the tabernacle of the testimony.*

Num 10:12 The children of Israel went forward according to their journeys out of the wilderness of Sinai; and the cloud stayed in the wilderness of Paran.

Num 10:13 They first went forward according to the commandment of YHWH by Moses.

Num 10:14 First, the standard of the camp of the children of Judah went forward according to their armies. Nahshon the son of Amminadab was over his army.

Num 10:15 Nethanel the son of Zuar was over the army of the tribe of the children of Issachar.

Num 10:16 Eliab the son of Helon was over the army of the tribe of the children of Zebulun.

Num 10:17 The tabernacle was taken down; and the sons of Gershon and the sons of Merari, who bore the tabernacle, went forward.

Num 10:18 The standard of the camp of Reuben went forward according to their armies. Elizur the son of Shedeur was over his army.

Num 10:19 Shelumiel the son of Zurishaddai was over the army of the tribe of the children of Simeon.

Num 10:20 Eliasaph the son of Deuel was over the army of the tribe of the children of Gad.

Num 10:21 The Kohathites set forward, bearing the sanctuary. The others set up the tabernacle before they arrived.

Num 10:22 The standard of the camp of the children of Ephraim set forward according to their armies. Elishama the son of Ammihud was over his army.

Num 10:23 Gamaliel the son of Pedahzur was over the army of the tribe of the children of Manasseh.

Num 10:24 Abidan the son of Gideoni was over the army of the tribe of the children of Benjamin.

Num 10:25 The standard of the camp of the children of Dan, which was the rear guard of all the camps, set forward according to their armies. Ahiezer the son of Ammishaddai was over his army.

MY NOTES

Num 10:26 Pagiel the son of Ochran was over the army of the tribe of the children of Asher.

Num 10:27 Ahira the son of Enan was over the army of the tribe of the children of Naphtali.

Num 10:28 Thus were the travels of the children of Israel according to their armies; and they went forward.

Num 10:29 Moses said to Hobab, the son of Reuel the Midianite, Moses' father-in-law, "We are journeying to the place of which YHWH said, 'I will give it to you.' Come with us, and we will treat you well; for YHWH has spoken good concerning Israel."

Num 10:30 He said to him, "I will not go; but I will depart to my own land, and to my relatives."

Num 10:31 He said, "Don't leave us, please; because you know how we are to encamp in the wilderness, and you can be our eyes.

Num 10:32 It shall be, if you go with us, yes, it shall be, that whatever good YHWH does to us, we will do the same to you."

Num 10:33 They set forward from the Mount of YHWH three days' journey. The ark of YHWH's covenant went before them three days' journey, to seek out a resting place for them.

Num 10:34 The cloud of YHWH was over them by day, when they set forward from the camp.

FRIDAY Num 10:35 When the ark went forward, Moses said, "Rise up, YHWH, and let your enemies be scattered! Let those who hate you flee before you!"

Num 10:36 When it rested, he said, "Return, YHWH, to the ten thousands of the thousands of Israel."

The People Complain

Num 11:1 *The people were complaining in the ears of YHWH. When YHWH heard it, his anger burned; and YHWH's fire burned among them, and consumed some of the outskirts of the camp.*

Num 11:2 The people cried to Moses; and Moses prayed to YHWH, and the fire abated.

Num 11:3 The name of that place was called Taberah, because YHWH's fire burned among them.

Num 11:4 The mixed multitude that was among them lusted exceedingly: and the children of Israel also wept again, and said, "Who will give us meat to eat?

Num 11:5 We remember the fish, which we ate in Egypt for nothing; the cucumbers, and the melons, and the leeks, and the onions, and the garlic;

MY NOTES

Num 11:6 but now we have lost our appetite. There is nothing at all except this manna to look at."

Num 11:7 The manna was like coriander seed, and its appearance like the appearance of bdellium.

Num 11:8 The people went around, gathered it, and ground it in mills, or beat it in mortars, and boiled it in pots, and made cakes of it. Its taste was like the taste of fresh oil.

Num 11:9 When the dew fell on the camp in the night, the manna fell on it.

Num 11:10 Moses heard the people weeping throughout their families, every man at the door of his tent; and YHWH's anger burned greatly; and Moses was displeased.

Num 11:11 Moses said to YHWH, "Why have you treated your servant so badly? Why haven't I found favor in your sight, that you lay the burden of all this people on me?

Num 11:12 Have I conceived all this people? Have I brought them out, that you should tell me, 'Carry them in your bosom, as a nurse carries a nursing infant, to the land which you swore to their fathers?'

Num 11:13 Where could I get meat to give all these people? For they weep before me, saying, 'Give us meat, that we may eat.'

Num 11:14 I am not able to bear all this people alone, because it is too heavy for me.

Num 11:15 If you treat me this way, please kill me right now, if I have found favor in your sight; and don't let me see my wretchedness."

Elders Appointed to Aid Moses

Num 11:16 YHWH said to Moses, "Gather to me seventy men of the elders of Israel, whom you know to be the elders of the people, and officers over them; and bring them to the Tent of Meeting, that they may stand there with you.

Num 11:17 I will come down and talk with you there. I will take of the Spirit which is on you, and will put it on them; and they shall bear the burden of the people with you, that you don't bear it yourself alone.

Num 11:18 "Say to the people, 'Sanctify yourselves in preparation for tomorrow, and you will eat meat; for you have wept in the ears of YHWH, saying, "Who will give us meat to eat? For it was well with us in Egypt." Therefore YHWH will give you meat, and you will eat.

Num 11:19 You will not eat one day, nor two days, nor five days, neither ten days, nor twenty days,

Num 11:20 but a whole month, until it comes out at your nostrils, and it is loathsome to you; because you have rejected YHWH who is among you, and have wept before him, saying, "Why did we come out of Egypt?"'"

MY NOTES

Num 11:21 Moses said, "The people, among whom I am, are six hundred thousand men on foot; and you have said, 'I will give them meat, that they may eat a whole month.'

Num 11:22 Shall flocks and herds be slaughtered for them, to be sufficient for them? Shall all the fish of the sea be gathered together for them, to be sufficient for them?"

Num 11:23 YHWH said to Moses, "Has YHWH's hand grown short? Now you will see whether my word will happen to you or not."

Num 11:24 Moses went out, and told the people YHWH's words; and he gathered seventy men of the elders of the people, and set them around the Tent.

Num 11:25 YHWH came down in the cloud, and spoke to him, and took of the Spirit that was on him, and put it on the seventy elders. When the Spirit rested on them, they prophesied, but they did so no more.

Num 11:26 But two men remained in the camp. The name of one was Eldad, and the name of the other Medad: and the Spirit rested on them; and they were of those who were written, but had not gone out to the Tent; and they prophesied in the camp.

Num 11:27 A young man ran, and told Moses, and said, "Eldad and Medad are prophesying in the camp!"

Num 11:28 Joshua the son of Nun, the servant of Moses, one of his chosen men, answered, "My lord Moses, forbid them!"

Num 11:29 Moses said to him, "Are you jealous for my sake? I wish that all YHWH's people were prophets, that YHWH would put his Spirit on them!"

SABBATH Num 11:30 Moses went into the camp, he and the elders of Israel.

Quail and a Plague

Num 11:31 A wind from YHWH went out and brought quails from the sea, and let them fall by the camp, about a day's journey on this side, and a day's journey on the other side, around the camp, and about two cubits above the surface of the earth.

Num 11:32 The people rose up all that day, and all of that night, and all the next day, and gathered the quails. He who gathered least gathered ten homers; and they spread them all out for themselves around the camp.

Num 11:33 While the meat was still between their teeth, before it was chewed, YHWH's anger burned against the people, and YHWH struck the people with a very great plague.

Num 11:34 The name of that place was called Kibroth Hattaavah, because there they buried the people who lusted.

Num 11:35 From Kibroth Hattaavah the people traveled to Hazeroth; and they stayed at Hazeroth.

MY NOTES

Miriam and Aaron Oppose Moses

Num 12:1 Miriam and Aaron spoke against Moses because of the Cushite woman whom he had married; for he had married a Cushite woman.

Num 12:2 They said, "Has YHWH indeed spoken only with Moses? Hasn't he spoken also with us?" And YHWH heard it.

Num 12:3 Now the man Moses was very humble, more than all the men who were on the surface of the earth.

Num 12:4 YHWH spoke suddenly to Moses, to Aaron, and to Miriam, "You three come out to the Tent of Meeting!" The three of them came out.

Num 12:5 YHWH came down in a pillar of cloud, and stood at the door of the Tent, and called Aaron and Miriam; and they both came forward.

Num 12:6 He said, "Now hear my words. If there is a prophet among you, I, YHWH, will make myself known to him in a vision. I will speak with him in a dream.

Num 12:7 My servant Moses is not so. He is faithful in all my house.

Num 12:8 With him, I will speak mouth to mouth, even plainly, and not in riddles; and he shall see YHWH's form. Why then were you not afraid to speak against my servant, against Moses?"

Num 12:9 YHWH's anger burned against them; and he departed.

Num 12:10 The cloud departed from over the Tent; and behold, Miriam was leprous, as white as snow. Aaron looked at Miriam, and behold, she was leprous.

Num 12:11 Aaron said to Moses, "Oh, my lord, please don't count this sin against us, in which we have done foolishly, and in which we have sinned.

Num 12:12 Let her not, I pray, be as one dead, of whom the flesh is half consumed when he comes out of his mother's womb."

Num 12:13 ***Moses cried to YHWH, saying, "Heal her, God, I beg you!"***

Num 12:14 YHWH said to Moses, "If her father had but spit in her face, shouldn't she be ashamed seven days? Let her be shut up outside of the camp seven days, and after that she shall be brought in again."

Num 12:15 Miriam was shut up outside of the camp seven days, and the people didn't travel until Miriam was brought in again.

Num 12:16 ***Afterward the people traveled from Hazeroth, and encamped in the wilderness of Paran.***

MY NOTES

Beha'alotekha CROSSWORD

Across
1. covered the tabernacle
3. Moses' sister
6. the material trumpets were made of
7. what happened to Miriam
9. people in charge of the tabernacle
10. age of retirement
11. 14th day of the first month

Down
1. when people are unhappy they do this
2. a type of bird
4. descendants of Jacob
5. Moses' brother
8. number of lamps Moses told Aaron to light

CRYPTOGRAM - Luke 17:27

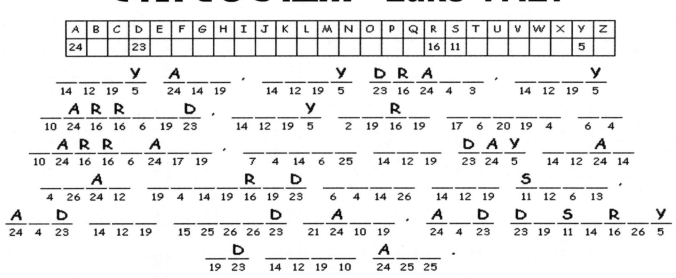

SHLACH

שְׁלַח or שְׁלַח-לְךָ

NUMBERS

It Means: **SEND FOR YOURSELF**

Our Thirty-Seventh Torah Portion is called Shlach! שְׁלַח-לְךָ
Numbers 13:1 – Numbers 15:41
PROPHETS: Joshua 2; Psalm 95; Ezekiel 20
NEW TESTAMENT: Mark 10:1-45; Hebrews 3:7-19

MAKE A MARK
Each time you hear someone say one of the words below make a '**/**" beside the word. See how many marks you can get!

grapes	
spy	
land	
goat	
tzitzit	
fringes	

FIRST FIND

~

If someone mentions a verse or scripture that is NOT in this Torah Portion, see if YOU can be the First to Find it!

This Weeks Torah Portion is:

Parsha: _____

Scriptures: _____

My Favorite Song was:

_____

date: _____

I talked to _____
about Today's Study.

Name: _____

words I didn't Understand

?!

The Most IMPORTANT
thing I Learned today was:

MY NOTES

Draw something you learned today

page 50

✓ I brought My Bible with me ☐
I am sitting with my Family ☐
I am ready to listen Carefully ☐

Spies Sent into Canaan

SUNDAY Num 13:1 YHWH spoke to Moses, saying,

Num 13:2 *"Send men, that they may spy out the land of Canaan, which I give to the children of Israel. Of every tribe of their fathers, you shall send a man, every one a prince among them."*

Num 13:3 Moses sent them from the wilderness of Paran according to the commandment of YHWH. All of them were men who were heads of the children of Israel.

Num 13:4 These were their names: Of the tribe of Reuben, Shammua the son of Zaccur.

Num 13:5 Of the tribe of Simeon, Shaphat the son of Hori.

Num 13:6 Of the tribe of Judah, Caleb the son of Jephunneh.

Num 13:7 Of the tribe of Issachar, Igal the son of Joseph.

Num 13:8 Of the tribe of Ephraim, Hoshea the son of Nun.

Num 13:9 Of the tribe of Benjamin, Palti the son of Raphu.

Num 13:10 Of the tribe of Zebulun, Gaddiel the son of Sodi.

Num 13:11 Of the tribe of Joseph, of the tribe of Manasseh, Gaddi the son of Susi.

Num 13:12 Of the tribe of Dan, Ammiel the son of Gemalli.

Num 13:13 Of the tribe of Asher, Sethur the son of Michael.

Num 13:14 Of the tribe of Naphtali, Nahbi the son of Vophsi.

Num 13:15 Of the tribe of Gad, Geuel the son of Machi.

Num 13:16 These are the names of the men who Moses sent to spy out the land. Moses called Hoshea the son of Nun Joshua.

Num 13:17 Moses sent them to spy out the land of Canaan, and said to them, "Go up this way by the South, and go up into the hill country.

Num 13:18 See the land, what it is; and the people who dwell therein, whether they are strong or weak, whether they are few or many;

Num 13:19 and what the land is that they dwell in, whether it is good or bad; and what cities they are that they dwell in, whether in camps, or in strongholds;

Num 13:20 and what the land is, whether it is fat or lean, whether there is wood therein, or not. Be courageous, and bring some of the fruit of the land." Now the time was the time of the first-ripe grapes.

MONDAY Num 13:21 So they went up, and spied out the land from the wilderness of Zin to Rehob, to the entrance of Hamath.

Num 13:22 They went up by the South, and came to Hebron; and Ahiman, Sheshai, and Talmai, the children of Anak, were there. (Now Hebron was built seven years before Zoan in Egypt.)

Num 13:23 They came to the valley of Eshcol, and cut down from there a branch with one cluster of grapes, and they bore it on a staff between two. They also brought some of the pomegranates and figs.

Num 13:24 That place was called the valley of Eshcol, because of the cluster which the children of Israel cut down from there.

Report of the Spies

Num 13:25 They returned from spying out the land at the end of forty days.

Num 13:26 They went and came to Moses, to Aaron, and to all the congregation of the children of Israel, to the wilderness of Paran, to Kadesh; and brought back word to them and to all the congregation. They showed them the fruit of the land.

Num 13:27 They told him, and said, "We came to the land where you sent us. Surely it flows with milk and honey, and this is its fruit.

Num 13:28 However the people who dwell in the land are strong, and the cities are fortified and very large. Moreover, we saw the children of Anak there.

Num 13:29 Amalek dwells in the land of the South. The Hittite, the Jebusite, and the Amorite dwell in the hill country. The Canaanite dwells by the sea, and along the side of the Jordan."

Num 13:30 Caleb stilled the people before Moses, and said, "Let's go up at once, and possess it; for we are well able to overcome it!"

Num 13:31 But the men who went up with him said, "We aren't able to go up against the people; for they are stronger than we."

Num 13:32 They brought up an evil report of the land which they had spied out to the children of Israel, saying, "The land, through which we have gone to spy it out, is a land that eats up its inhabitants; and all the people who we saw in it are men of great stature.

Num 13:33 There we saw the Nephilim, the sons of Anak, who come from the Nephilim. We were in our own sight as grasshoppers, and so we were in their sight."

The People Rebel

Num 14:1 All the congregation lifted up their voice, and cried; and the people wept that night.

Num 14:2 **All the children of Israel murmured against Moses and against Aaron. The whole congregation said to them, "We wish that we had died in the land of Egypt, or that we had died in this wilderness!**

Num 14:3 Why does YHWH bring us to this land, to fall by the sword? Our wives and our little ones will be captured or killed! Wouldn't it be better for us to return into Egypt?"

MY NOTES

Num 14:4 They said to one another, "Let's make a captain, and let's return into Egypt."

Num 14:5 Then Moses and Aaron fell on their faces before all the assembly of the congregation of the children of Israel.

Num 14:6 Joshua the son of Nun and Caleb the son of Jephunneh, who were of those who spied out the land, tore their clothes.

Num 14:7 They spoke to all the congregation of the children of Israel, saying, "The land, which we passed through to spy it out, is an exceeding good land.

TUESDAY Num 14:8 If YHWH delights in us, then he will bring us into this land, and give it to us; a land which flows with milk and honey.

Num 14:9 Only don't rebel against YHWH, neither fear the people of the land; for they are bread for us. Their defense is removed from over them, and YHWH is with us. Don't fear them."

Num 14:10 But all the congregation threatened to stone them with stones. YHWH's glory appeared in the Tent of Meeting to all the children of Israel.

Num 14:11 YHWH said to Moses, "How long will this people despise me? and how long will they not believe in me, for all the signs which I have worked among them?

Num 14:12 I will strike them with the pestilence, and disinherit them, and will make of you a nation greater and mightier than they."

Moses Intercedes for the People

Num 14:13 Moses said to YHWH, "Then the Egyptians will hear it; for you brought up this people in your might from among them.

Num 14:14 They will tell it to the inhabitants of this land. They have heard that you YHWH are among this people; for you YHWH are seen face to face, and your cloud stands over them, and you go before them, in a pillar of cloud by day, and in a pillar of fire by night.

Num 14:15 Now if you killed this people as one man, then the nations which have heard the fame of you will speak, saying,

Num 14:16 'Because YHWH was not able to bring this people into the land which he swore to them, therefore he has slain them in the wilderness.'

Num 14:17 Now please let the power of the Lord be great, according as you have spoken, saying,

MY NOTES

Num 14:18 *'YHWH is slow to anger, and abundant in loving kindness, forgiving iniquity and disobedience; and he will by no means clear the guilty, visiting the iniquity of the fathers on the children, on the third and on the fourth generation.'*

Num 14:19 Please pardon the iniquity of this people according to the greatness of your loving kindness, and just as you have forgiven this people, from Egypt even until now."

God Promises Judgment

Num 14:20 YHWH said, "I have pardoned according to your word:

Num 14:21 but in very deed, as I live, and as all the earth shall be filled with YHWH's glory;

Num 14:22 because all those men who have seen my glory, and my signs, which I worked in Egypt and in the wilderness, yet have tempted me these ten times, and have not listened to my voice;

Num 14:23 surely they shall not see the land which I swore to their fathers, neither shall any of those who despised me see it.

Num 14:24 But my servant Caleb, because he had another spirit with him, and has followed me fully, him I will bring into the land into which he went. His offspring shall possess it.

Num 14:25 Since the Amalekite and the Canaanite dwell in the valley, tomorrow turn, and go into the wilderness by the way to the Red Sea."

WEDNESDAY Num 14:26 YHWH spoke to Moses and to Aaron, saying,

Num 14:27 "How long shall I bear with this evil congregation, that murmur against me? I have heard the murmurings of the children of Israel, which they murmur against me.

Num 14:28 Tell them, 'As I live, says YHWH, surely as you have spoken in my ears, so I will do to you.

Num 14:29 Your dead bodies shall fall in this wilderness; and all who were counted of you, according to your whole number, from twenty years old and upward, who have murmured against me,

Num 14:30 surely you shall not come into the land, concerning which I swore that I would make you dwell therein, except Caleb the son of Jephunneh, and Joshua the son of Nun.

Num 14:31 *But your little ones, that you said should be captured or killed, them I will bring in, and they shall know the land which you have rejected.*

Num 14:32 But as for you, your dead bodies shall fall in this wilderness.

Num 14:33 Your children shall be wanderers in the wilderness forty years, and shall bear your prostitution, until your dead bodies are consumed in the wilderness.

Num 14:34 After the number of the days in which you spied out the land, even forty days, for every day a year, you will bear your iniquities, even forty years, and you will know my alienation.'

Num 14:35 I, YHWH, have spoken. I will surely do this to all this evil congregation, who are gathered together against me. In this wilderness they shall be consumed, and there they shall die."

Num 14:36 The men, whom Moses sent to spy out the land, who returned, and made all the congregation to murmur against him, by bringing up an evil report against the land,

Num 14:37 even those men who brought up an evil report of the land, died by the plague before YHWH.

Num 14:38 But Joshua the son of Nun, and Caleb the son of Jephunneh, remained alive of those men who went to spy out the land.

Israel Defeated in Battle

Num 14:39 Moses told these words to all the children of Israel, and the people mourned greatly.

Num 14:40 They rose up early in the morning, and went up to the top of the mountain, saying, "Behold, we are here, and will go up to the place which YHWH has promised: for we have sinned."

Num 14:41 Moses said, "Why now do you disobey the commandment of YHWH, since it shall not prosper?

Num 14:42 Don't go up, for YHWH isn't among you; that way you won't be struck down before your enemies.

Num 14:43 For there the Amalekite and the Canaanite are before you, and you will fall by the sword, because you turned back from following YHWH, therefore YHWH will not be with you."

Num 14:44 But they presumed to go up to the top of the mountain. Nevertheless, the ark of YHWH's covenant and Moses didn't depart out of the camp.

Num 14:45 Then the Amalekites came down, and the Canaanites who lived in that mountain, and struck them and beat them down, even to Hormah.

Laws About Sacrifices

Num 15:1 YHWH spoke to Moses, saying,

Num 15:2 "Speak to the children of Israel, and tell them, 'When you have come into the land of your habitations, which I give to you,

Num 15:3 and will make an offering by fire to YHWH, a burnt offering, or a sacrifice, to accomplish a vow, or as a freewill offering, or in your set feasts, to make a pleasant aroma to YHWH, of the herd, or of the flock;

Num 15:4 then he who offers his offering shall offer to YHWH a meal offering of one tenth of an ephah of fine flour mixed with the fourth part of a hin of oil.

Num 15:5 You shall prepare wine for the drink offering, the fourth part of a hin, with the burnt offering, or for the sacrifice, for each lamb.

Num 15:6 "'Or for a ram, you shall prepare for a meal offering two tenths of an ephah of fine flour mixed with the third part of a hin of oil;

Num 15:7 and for the drink offering you shall offer the third part of a hin of wine, of a pleasant aroma to YHWH.

THURSDAY Num 15:8 When you prepare a bull for a burnt offering, or for a sacrifice, to accomplish a vow, or for peace offerings to YHWH;

Num 15:9 then shall he offer with the bull a meal offering of three tenths of an ephah of fine flour mixed with half a hin of oil:

Num 15:10 and you shall offer for the drink offering half a hin of wine, for an offering made by fire, of a pleasant aroma to YHWH.

Num 15:11 Thus shall it be done for each bull, or for each ram, or for each of the male lambs, or of the young goats.

Num 15:12 According to the number that you shall prepare, so you shall do to everyone according to their number.

Num 15:13 "'All who are native-born shall do these things in this way, in offering an offering made by fire, of a pleasant aroma to YHWH.

Num 15:14 If a stranger lives as a foreigner with you, or whoever may be among you throughout your generations, and will offer an offering made by fire, of a pleasant aroma to YHWH; as you do, so he shall do.

Num 15:15 *For the assembly, there shall be one statute for you and for the stranger who lives as a foreigner, a statute forever throughout your generations. As you are, so shall the foreigner be before YHWH.*

Num 15:16 One law and one ordinance shall be for you, and for the stranger who lives as a foreigner with you.'"

FRIDAY Num 15:17 YHWH spoke to Moses, saying,

Num 15:18 "Speak to the children of Israel, and tell them, 'When you come into the land where I bring you,

Num 15:19 then it shall be that when you eat of the bread of the land, you shall offer up a wave offering to YHWH.

MY NOTES

page 57

Num 15:20 Of the first of your dough you shall offer up a cake for a wave offering. As the wave offering of the threshing floor, so you shall heave it.

Num 15:21 Of the first of your dough, you shall give to YHWH a wave offering throughout your generations.

Laws About Unintentional Sins

Num 15:22 "'When you err, and don't observe all these commandments, which YHWH has spoken to Moses,

Num 15:23 even all that YHWH has commanded you by Moses, from the day that YHWH gave commandment, and onward throughout your generations;

Num 15:24 then it shall be, if it was done unwittingly, without the knowledge of the congregation, that all the congregation shall offer one young bull for a burnt offering, for a pleasant aroma to YHWH, with its meal offering, and its drink offering, according to the ordinance, and one male goat for a sin offering.

Num 15:25 The priest shall make atonement for all the congregation of the children of Israel, and they shall be forgiven; for it was an error, and they have brought their offering, an offering made by fire to YHWH, and their sin offering before YHWH, for their error.

Num 15:26 *All the congregation of the children of Israel shall be forgiven, as well as the stranger who lives as a foreigner among them; for with regard to all the people, it was done unwittingly.*

SABBATH Num 15:27 "'If one person sins unwittingly, then he shall offer a female goat a year old for a sin offering.

Num 15:28 The priest shall make atonement for the soul who errs, when he sins unwittingly before YHWH, to make atonement for him; and he shall be forgiven.

Num 15:29 You shall have one law for him who does anything unwittingly, for him who is native-born among the children of Israel, and for the stranger who lives as a foreigner among them.

Num 15:30 "'But the soul who does anything with a high hand, whether he is native-born or a foreigner, the same blasphemes YHWH. That soul shall be cut off from among his people.

Num 15:31 *Because he has despised YHWH's word, and has broken his commandment, that soul shall utterly be cut off. His iniquity shall be on him.'"*

A Sabbathbreaker Executed

Num 15:32 While the children of Israel were in the wilderness, they found a man gathering sticks on the Sabbath day.

Num 15:33 Those who found him gathering sticks brought him to Moses and Aaron, and to all the congregation.

Num 15:34 They put him in custody, because it had not been declared what should be done to him.

Num 15:35 YHWH said to Moses, "The man shall surely be put to death. All the congregation shall stone him with stones outside of the camp."

Num 15:36 All the congregation brought him outside of the camp, and stoned him to death with stones, as YHWH commanded Moses.

Tassels on Garments

Num 15:37 YHWH spoke to Moses, saying,

Num 15:38 ***"Speak to the children of Israel, and tell them that they should make themselves fringes in the borders of their garments throughout their generations, and that they put on the fringe of each border a cord of blue:***

Num 15:39 and it shall be to you for a fringe, that you may look on it, and remember all YHWH's commandments, and do them; and that you don' t follow your own heart and your own eyes, after which you use to play the prostitute;

Num 15:40 so that you may remember and do all my commandments, and be holy to your God.

Num 15:41 I am YHWH your God, who brought you out of the land of Egypt, to be your God: I am YHWH your God."

MY NOTES

_____
_____
_____
_____
_____
_____
_____
_____
_____
_____
_____
_____
_____

VERSE FIND – PSALM 95:1

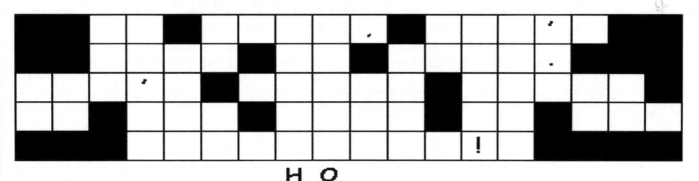

bible books WORD FIND

```
W  L  X  J  S  E  T  S  A  I  S  E  L  C  C  E  J  Q  Y  T
T  H  A  I  N  A  H  P  E  Z  W  F  K  U  K  K  A  B  A  H
C  A  E  M  R  Q  J  J  H  E  G  Q  C  H  E  B  R  E  W  S
S  Y  T  Z  E  Z  B  B  T  S  U  C  I  T  I  V  E  L  D  F
N  P  E  R  G  N  O  S  S  I  R  P  S  H  W  L  Z  N  J  R
A  R  S  S  F  U  T  P  K  E  Y  W  S  I  S  E  N  E  G  P
I  O  E  N  G  A  F  A  V  R  D  S  S  A  C  D  N  D  B  H
S  V  G  A  A  O  C  E  T  S  A  I  Y  H  Y  Q  F  S  A  H
S  E  D  I  T  H  L  T  O  I  W  M  A  E  Z  E  K  I  E  L
O  R  U  P  N  A  A  M  S  E  O  R  B  G  D  E  D  U  J  H
L  B  J  P  T  G  A  N  H  N  I  N  P  T  G  A  M  O  C  A
O  S  A  I  R  A  T  T  O  A  Z  W  S  E  B  H  Q  H  H  I
C  K  O  L  L  T  R  H  J  O  D  C  O  B  I  K  E  R  A
Z  N  B  I  W  A  E  J  M  M  L  E  I  N  A  D  R  X  O  S
V  E  I  H  M  T  S  N  A  I  H  T  N  I  R  O  C  O  N  I
H  K  A  P  U  I  V  P  H  I  L  E  M  O  N  B  H  D  I  L
Z  U  Z  E  B  A  W  D  H  A  I  M  E  H  E  N  S  U  C  I
I  L  D  L  L  N  G  G  N  I  A  G  G  A  H  S  E  S  L  F
C  R  N  V  F  S  O  N  G  S  S  N  A  I  S  E  H  P  E  D
G  S  S  R  E  B  M  U  N  J  E  R  E  M  I  A  H  G  S  H
```

ACTS	AMOS	CHRONICLES
COLOSSIANS	CORINTHIANS	DANIEL
DEUTERONOMY	ECCLESIASTES	EPHESIANS
EZEKIEL	EZRA	GALATIANS
GENESIS	HABAKKUK	HAGGAI
HEBREWS	ISAIAH	JEREMIAH
JONAH	JUDE	LAMENTATIONS
LEVITICUS	MARK	MATTHEW
NEHEMIAH	OBADIAH	PHILEMON
PHILIPPIANS	PROVERBS	REVELATION
SONG	OF	SONGS
ZECHARIAH	ZEPHANIAH	LUKE
EXODUS	NUMBERS	JUDGES

KORACH

קֹרַח

NUMBERS

It Means: **BALDNESS**

Our Thirty-Eighth Torah Portion is called Korach! קֹרַח
Numbers 16:1 – Numbers 18:32
PROPHETS: 1 Samuel 11:14-12:22
NEW TESTAMENT: Luke 18:35–19:28; Romans 13:1-7; 2 Timothy 2:8-21; Jude

MAKE A MARK
Each time you hear someone say one of the words below
make a '/" beside the word. See how many marks you can get!

Korah	
plague	
Aaron	
staff	
bloom	
tithe	

FIRST FIND

~

If someone mentions a verse or scripture that is NOT in this Torah
Portion, see if YOU can be the First to Find it!

This Weeks Torah Portion is:

Parsha: _____

Scriptures: _____

Name: _____

words I didn't Understand

?!

My Favorite Song was:

date: _____

I talked to _____
about Today's Study.

The Most IMPORTANT
thing I Learned today was:

MY NOTES

Draw something you learned today

I brought My Bible with me ☐
✓ I am sitting with my Family ☐
I am ready to listen Carefully ☐

Korah's Rebellion

SUNDAY Num 16:1 Now Korah, the son of Izhar, the son of Kohath, the son of Levi, with Dathan and Abiram, the sons of Eliab, and On, the son of Peleth, sons of Reuben, took some men.

Num 16:2 They rose up before Moses, with some of the children of Israel, two hundred fifty princes of the congregation, called to the assembly, men of renown.

Num 16:3 They assembled themselves together against Moses and against Aaron, and said to them, "You take too much on yourself, since all the congregation are holy, everyone of them, and YHWH is among them! Why do you lift yourselves up above YHWH's assembly?"

Num 16:4 When Moses heard it, he fell on his face.

Num 16:5 *He said to Korah and to all his company, "In the morning, YHWH will show who are his, and who is holy, and will cause him to come near to him. Even him whom he shall choose, he will cause to come near to him.*

Num 16:6 Do this: take censers, Korah, and all his company;

Num 16:7 and put fire in them, and put incense on them before YHWH tomorrow. It shall be that the man whom YHWH chooses, he shall be holy. You have gone too far, you sons of Levi!"

Num 16:8 Moses said to Korah, "Hear now, you sons of Levi!

Num 16:9 Is it a small thing to you, that the God of Israel has separated you from the congregation of Israel, to bring you near to himself, to do the service of YHWH's tabernacle, and to stand before the congregation to minister to them;

Num 16:10 and that he has brought you near, and all your brothers the sons of Levi with you? Do you seek the priesthood also?

Num 16:11 Therefore you and all your company have gathered together against YHWH! What is Aaron that you murmur against him?"

Num 16:12 Moses sent to call Dathan and Abiram, the sons of Eliab; and they said, "We won't come up!

Num 16:13 Is it a small thing that you have brought us up out of a land flowing with milk and honey, to kill us in the wilderness, but you must also make yourself a prince over us?

MONDAY Num 16:14 Moreover you haven't brought us into a land flowing with milk and honey, nor given us inheritance of fields and vineyards. Will you put out the eyes of these men? We won't come up."

MY NOTES

Num 16:15 ***Moses was very angry, and said to YHWH, "Don't respect their offering. I have not taken one donkey from them, neither have I hurt one of them."***

Num 16:16 Moses said to Korah, "You and all your company go before YHWH, you, and they, and Aaron, tomorrow.

Num 16:17 Each man take his censer, and put incense on them, and each man bring before YHWH his censer, two hundred fifty censers; you also, and Aaron, each his censer."

Num 16:18 They each took his censer, and put fire in them, and laid incense on it, and stood at the door of the Tent of Meeting with Moses and Aaron.

Num 16:19 Korah assembled all the congregation opposite them to the door of the Tent of Meeting. YHWH's glory appeared to all the congregation.

TUESDAY Num 16:20 YHWH spoke to Moses and to Aaron, saying,

Num 16:21 "Separate yourselves from among this congregation, that I may consume them in a moment!"

Num 16:22 They fell on their faces, and said, "God, the God of the spirits of all flesh, shall one man sin, and will you be angry with all the congregation?"

Num 16:23 YHWH spoke to Moses, saying,

Num 16:24 "Speak to the congregation, saying, 'Get away from around the tent of Korah, Dathan, and Abiram!'"

Num 16:25 Moses rose up and went to Dathan and Abiram; and the elders of Israel followed him.

Num 16:26 ***He spoke to the congregation, saying, "Depart, please, from the tents of these wicked men, and touch nothing of theirs, lest you be consumed in all their sins!"***

Num 16:27 So they went away from the tent of Korah, Dathan, and Abiram, on every side. Dathan and Abiram came out, and stood at the door of their tents, with their wives, their sons, and their little ones.

Num 16:28 Moses said, "Hereby you shall know that YHWH has sent me to do all these works; for they are not from my own mind.

Num 16:29 If these men die the common death of all men, or if they experience what all men experience, then YHWH hasn't sent me.

Num 16:30 But if YHWH makes a new thing, and the ground opens its mouth, and swallows them up, with all that belong to them, and they go down alive into Sheol; then you shall understand that these men have despised YHWH."

Num 16:31 As he finished speaking all these words, the ground that was under them split apart.

MY NOTES

_____
_____
_____
_____
_____
_____
_____
_____
_____
_____
_____
_____
_____
_____
_____
_____
_____
_____
_____
_____
_____
_____
_____
_____
_____
_____
_____
_____
_____

Num 16:32 The earth opened its mouth and swallowed them up, with their households, all of Korah's men, and all their goods.

Num 16:33 So they, and all that belonged to them went down alive into Sheol. The earth closed on them, and they perished from among the assembly.

Num 16:34 All Israel that were around them fled at their cry; for they said, "Lest the earth swallow us up!"

Num 16:35 Fire came out from YHWH, and devoured the two hundred fifty men who offered the incense.

WEDNESDAY Num 16:36 YHWH spoke to Moses, saying,

Num 16:37 "Speak to Eleazar the son of Aaron the priest, that he take up the censers out of the burning, and scatter the fire away from the camp; for they are holy,

Num 16:38 even the censers of those who sinned against their own lives. Let them be beaten into plates for a covering of the altar, for they offered them before YHWH. Therefore they are holy. They shall be a sign to the children of Israel."

Num 16:39 Eleazar the priest took the bronze censers, which those who were burned had offered; and they beat them out for a covering of the altar,

Num 16:40 to be a memorial to the children of Israel, to the end that no stranger, who isn't of the offspring of Aaron, would come near to burn incense before YHWH, that he not be as Korah, and as his company; as YHWH spoke to him by Moses.

Num 16:41 But on the next day all the congregation of the children of Israel murmured against Moses and against Aaron, saying, "You have killed YHWH's people!"

Num 16:42 When the congregation was assembled against Moses and against Aaron, They looked toward the Tent of Meeting. Behold, the cloud covered it, and YHWH's glory appeared.

Num 16:43 Moses and Aaron came to the front of the Tent of Meeting.

Num 16:44 YHWH spoke to Moses, saying,

Num 16:45 "Get away from among this congregation, that I may consume them in a moment!" They fell on their faces.

Num 16:46 Moses said to Aaron, "Take your censer, and put fire from off the altar in it, and lay incense on it, and carry it quickly to the congregation, and make atonement for them; for wrath has gone out from YHWH! The plague has begun."

Num 16:47 Aaron did as Moses said, and ran into the middle of the assembly. The plague had already begun among the people. He put on the incense, and made atonement for the people.

MY NOTES

Num 16:48 He stood between the dead and the living; and the plague was stayed.

Num 16:49 Now those who died by the plague were fourteen thousand and seven hundred, in addition to those who died about the matter of Korah.

Num 16:50 Aaron returned to Moses to the door of the Tent of Meeting, and the plague was stopped.

Aaron's Staff Buds

Num 17:1 YHWH spoke to Moses, saying,

Num 17:2 "Speak to the children of Israel, and take rods from them, one for each fathers' house, of all their princes according to their fathers' houses, twelve rods. Write each man's name on his rod.

Num 17:3 **You shall write Aaron's name on the rod of Levi; for there shall be one rod for each head of their fathers' houses.**

Num 17:4 You shall lay them up in the Tent of Meeting before the testimony, where I meet with you.

Num 17:5 It shall happen, that the rod of the man whom I shall choose shall bud. I will make the murmurings of the children of Israel, which they murmur against you, cease from me."

Num 17:6 Moses spoke to the children of Israel; and all their princes gave him rods, for each prince one, according to their fathers' houses, a total of twelve rods. Aaron's rod was among their rods.

Num 17:7 Moses laid up the rods before YHWH in the Tent of the Testimony.

Num 17:8 On the next day, Moses went into the Tent of the Testimony; and behold, Aaron's rod for the house of Levi had sprouted, budded, produced blossoms, and bore ripe almonds.

THURSDAY Num 17:9 Moses brought out all the rods from before YHWH to all the children of Israel. They looked, and each man took his rod.

Num 17:10 **YHWH said to Moses, "Put back the rod of Aaron before the testimony, to be kept for a token against the children of rebellion; that you may make an end of their murmurings against me, that they not die."**

Num 17:11 Moses did so. As YHWH commanded him, so he did.

Num 17:12 The children of Israel spoke to Moses, saying, "Behold, we perish! We are undone! We are all undone!

Num 17:13 Everyone who keeps approaching YHWH's tabernacle, dies! Will we all perish?"

MY NOTES

Duties of Priests and Levites

Num 18:1 YHWH said to Aaron, "You and your sons and your fathers' house with you shall bear the iniquity of the sanctuary; and you and your sons with you shall bear the iniquity of your priesthood.

Num 18:2 Bring your brothers also, the tribe of Levi, the tribe of your father, near with you, that they may be joined to you, and minister to you; but you and your sons with you shall be before the Tent of the Testimony.

Num 18:3 They shall keep your commands, and the duty of the whole Tent; only they shall not come near to the vessels of the sanctuary and to the altar, that they not die, neither they, nor you.

Num 18:4 They shall be joined to you, and keep the responsibility of the Tent of Meeting, for all the service of the Tent. A stranger shall not come near to you.

Num 18:5 "You shall perform the duty of the sanctuary and the duty of the altar, that there be no more wrath on the children of Israel.

Num 18:6 Behold, I myself have taken your brothers the Levites from among the children of Israel. They are a gift to you, dedicated to YHWH, to do the service of the Tent of Meeting.

Num 18:7 You and your sons with you shall keep your priesthood for everything of the altar, and for that within the veil. You shall serve. I give you the service of the priesthood as a gift. The stranger who comes near shall be put to death."

FRIDAY Num 18:8 *YHWH spoke to Aaron, "Behold, I myself have given you the command of my wave offerings, even all the holy things of the children of Israel. I have given them to you by reason of the anointing, and to your sons, as a portion forever.*

Num 18:9 This shall be yours of the most holy things from the fire: every offering of theirs, even every meal offering of theirs, and every sin offering of theirs, and every trespass offering of theirs, which they shall render to me, shall be most holy for you and for your sons.

Num 18:10 You shall eat of it like the most holy things. Every male shall eat of it. It shall be holy to you.

Num 18:11 "This is yours, too: the wave offering of their gift, even all the wave offerings of the children of Israel. I have given them to you, and to your sons and to your daughters with you, as a portion forever. Everyone who is clean in your house shall eat of it.

MY NOTES

Num 18:12 "I have given to you all the best of the oil, and all the best of the vintage, and of the grain, the first fruits of them which they give to YHWH.

Num 18:13 The first-ripe fruits of all that is in their land, which they bring to YHWH, shall be yours. Everyone who is clean in your house shall eat of it.

Num 18:14 "Everything devoted in Israel shall be yours.

Num 18:15 Everything that opens the womb, of all flesh which they offer to YHWH, both of man and animal shall be yours. Nevertheless, you shall surely redeem the firstborn of man, and you shall redeem the firstborn of unclean animals.

Num 18:16 You shall redeem those who are to be redeemed of them from a month old, according to your estimation, for five shekels of money, after the shekel of the sanctuary, which weighs twenty gerahs.

Num 18:17 "But you shall not redeem the firstborn of a cow, or the firstborn of a sheep, or the firstborn of a goat. They are holy. You shall sprinkle their blood on the altar, and shall burn their fat for an offering made by fire, for a pleasant aroma to YHWH.

Num 18:18 Their meat shall be yours, as the wave offering breast and as the right thigh, it shall be yours.

Num 18:19 All the wave offerings of the holy things, which the children of Israel offer to YHWH, I have given you, and your sons and your daughters with you, as a portion forever. It is a covenant of salt forever before YHWH to you and to your offspring with you."

SABBATH Num 18:20 YHWH said to Aaron, "You shall have no inheritance in their land, neither shall you have any portion among them. I am your portion and your inheritance among the children of Israel.

Num 18:21 "To the children of Levi, behold, I have given all the tithe in Israel for an inheritance, in return for their service which they serve, even the service of the Tent of Meeting.

Num 18:22 Henceforth the children of Israel shall not come near the Tent of Meeting, lest they bear sin, and die.

Num 18:23 But the Levites shall do the service of the Tent of Meeting, and they shall bear their iniquity. It shall be a statute forever throughout your generations. Among the children of Israel, they shall have no inheritance.

Num 18:24 For the tithe of the children of Israel, which they offer as a wave offering to YHWH, I have given to the Levites for an inheritance. Therefore I have said to them, 'Among the children of Israel they shall have no inheritance.'"

Num 18:25 YHWH spoke to Moses, saying,

MY NOTES

Num 18:26 *"Moreover you shall speak to the Levites, and tell them, 'When you take of the children of Israel the tithe which I have given you from them for your inheritance, then you shall offer up a wave offering of it for YHWH, a tithe of the tithe.*

Num 18:27 Your wave offering shall be credited to you, as though it were the grain of the threshing floor, and as the fullness of the wine press.

Num 18:28 Thus you also shall offer a wave offering to YHWH of all your tithes, which you receive of the children of Israel; and of it you shall give YHWH's wave offering to Aaron the priest.

Num 18:29 Out of all your gifts, you shall offer every wave offering of YHWH, of all its best parts, even the holy part of it.'

Num 18:30 "Therefore you shall tell them, 'When you heave its best from it, then it shall be credited to the Levites as the increase of the threshing floor, and as the increase of the wine press.

Num 18:31 You may eat it anywhere, you and your households, for it is your reward in return for your service in the Tent of Meeting.

Num 18:32 You shall bear no sin by reason of it, when you have heaved from it its best. You shall not profane the holy things of the children of Israel, that you not die.'"

MY NOTES

_____
_____
_____
_____
_____
_____
_____
_____
_____
_____
_____
_____
_____
_____
_____

VERSE FIND – 2 TIMOTHY 2:8

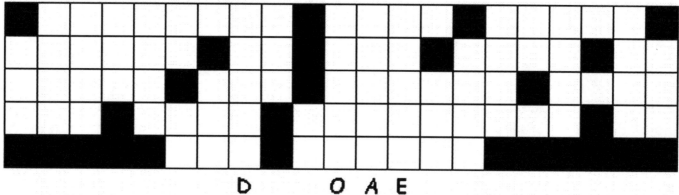

READ: LUKE 18:35–19:28
Help Zacchaeus out of the Tree

~BONUS~

What type of tree did Zacchaeus climb?

_____

Where did Zacchaeus take Yeshua?

_____

CHUKAT

חֻקַּת

NUMBERS

It Means: **LAW**

Our Thirty-Ninth Torah Portion is called Chukat! חֻקַּת
Numbers 19:1 – Numbers 22:1
PROPHETS: Judges 11:1-33; Isaiah 66:1-24
NEW TESTAMENT: Matthew 21:1-17; John 3:1-21; 4:3-30; 12:27-50

MAKE A MARK

Each time you hear someone say one of the words below make a '**/**" beside the word. See how many marks you can get!

calf	
hyssop	
Miriam	
rod	
serpent	
water	

FIRST FIND

~

If someone mentions a verse or scripture that is NOT in this Torah Portion, see if YOU can be the First to Find it!

This Weeks Torah Portion is:

Parsha: _____

Scriptures: _____

My Favorite Song was:

date: _____

I talked to _____
about Today's Study.

MY NOTES

Name: _____

Words I didn't Understand

The Most IMPORTANT thing I Learned today was:

Draw something you learned today

✓ I brought My Bible with me ☐
I am sitting with my Family ☐
I am ready to listen Carefully ☐

Laws for Purification

SUNDAY Num 19:1 YHWH spoke to Moses and to Aaron, saying,

Num 19:2 "This is the statute of the law which YHWH has commanded. Tell the children of Israel to bring you a red heifer without spot, in which is no defect, and which was never yoked.

Num 19:3 You shall give her to Eleazar the priest, and he shall bring her outside of the camp, and one shall kill her before his face.

Num 19:4 Eleazar the priest shall take some of her blood with his finger, and sprinkle her blood toward the front of the Tent of Meeting seven times.

Num 19:5 One shall burn the heifer in his sight; her skin, and her meat, and her blood, with her dung, shall he burn.

Num 19:6 The priest shall take cedar wood, hyssop, and scarlet, and cast it into the middle of the burning of the heifer.

Num 19:7 Then the priest shall wash his clothes, and he shall bathe his flesh in water, and afterward he shall come into the camp, and the priest shall be unclean until the evening.

Num 19:8 He who burns her shall wash his clothes in water, and bathe his flesh in water, and shall be unclean until the evening.

Num 19:9 "A man who is clean shall gather up the ashes of the heifer, and lay them up outside of the camp in a clean place; and it shall be kept for the congregation of the children of Israel for use in water for cleansing impurity. It is a sin offering.

Num 19:10 He who gathers the ashes of the heifer shall wash his clothes, and be unclean until the evening. It shall be to the children of Israel, and to the stranger who lives as a foreigner among them, for a statute forever.

Num 19:11 *"He who touches the dead body of any man shall be unclean seven days.*

Num 19:12 He shall purify himself with water on the third day, and on the seventh day he shall be clean; but if he doesn't purify himself the third day, then the seventh day he shall not be clean.

Num 19:13 Whoever touches a dead person, the body of a man who has died, and doesn't purify himself, defiles YHWH's tabernacle; and that soul shall be cut off from Israel; because the water for impurity was not sprinkled on him, he shall be unclean. His uncleanness is yet on him.

Num 19:14 "This is the law when a man dies in a tent: everyone who comes into the tent, and everyone who is in the tent, shall be unclean seven days.

Num 19:15 Every open vessel, which has no covering bound on it, is unclean.

Num 19:16 "Whoever in the open field touches one who is slain with a sword, or a dead body, or a bone of a man, or a grave, shall be unclean seven days.

Num 19:17 "For the unclean, they shall take of the ashes of the burning of the sin offering; and running water shall be poured into a vessel.

MONDAY Num 19:18 A clean person shall take hyssop, dip it in the water, and sprinkle it on the tent, on all the vessels, on the persons who were there, and on him who touched the bone, or the slain, or the dead, or the grave.

Num 19:19 The clean person shall sprinkle on the unclean on the third day, and on the seventh day. On the seventh day, he shall purify him. He shall wash his clothes and bathe himself in water, and shall be clean at evening.

Num 19:20 But the man who shall be unclean, and shall not purify himself, that soul shall be cut off from among the assembly, because he has defiled the sanctuary of YHWH. The water for impurity has not been sprinkled on him. He is unclean.

Num 19:21 It shall be a perpetual statute to them. He who sprinkles the water for impurity shall wash his clothes, and he who touches the water for impurity shall be unclean until evening.

Num 19:22 "Whatever the unclean person touches shall be unclean; and the soul that touches it shall be unclean until evening."

The Death of Miriam

Num 20:1 The children of Israel, even the whole congregation, came into the wilderness of Zin in the first month. The people stayed in Kadesh. Miriam died there, and was buried there.

The Waters of Meribah

Num 20:2 There was no water for the congregation; and they assembled themselves together against Moses and against Aaron.

Num 20:3 *The people quarreled with Moses, and spoke, saying, "We wish that we had died when our brothers died before YHWH!*

Num 20:4 Why have you brought YHWH's assembly into this wilderness, that we should die there, we and our animals?

Num 20:5 Why have you made us to come up out of Egypt, to bring us in to this evil place? It is no place of seed, or of figs, or of vines, or of pomegranates; neither is there any water to drink."

Num 20:6 Moses and Aaron went from the presence of the assembly to the door of the Tent of Meeting, and fell on their faces. YHWH's glory appeared to them.

TUESDAY Num 20:7 YHWH spoke to Moses, saying,

Num 20:8 *"Take the rod, and assemble the congregation, you, and Aaron your brother, and speak to the rock before their eyes, that it pour out its water. You shall bring water to them out of the rock; so you shall give the congregation and their livestock drink."*

Num 20:9 Moses took the rod from before YHWH, as he commanded him.

Moses Strikes the Rock

Num 20:10 Moses and Aaron gathered the assembly together before the rock, and he said to them, "Hear now, you rebels! Shall we bring water out of this rock for you?"

Num 20:11 *Moses lifted up his hand, and struck the rock with his rod twice, and water came out abundantly. The congregation and their livestock drank.*

Num 20:12 YHWH said to Moses and Aaron, "Because you didn't believe in me, to sanctify me in the eyes of the children of Israel, therefore you shall not bring this assembly into the land which I have given them."

Num 20:13 These are the waters of Meribah; because the children of Israel strove with YHWH, and he was sanctified in them.

Edom Refuses Passage

WEDNESDAY Num 20:14 Moses sent messengers from Kadesh to the king of Edom, saying: "Thus says your brother Israel: You know all the travail that has happened to us;

Num 20:15 how our fathers went down into Egypt, and we lived in Egypt a long time. The Egyptians mistreated us and our fathers.

Num 20:16 *When we cried to YHWH, he heard our voice, sent an angel, and brought us out of Egypt. Behold, we are in Kadesh, a city in the edge of your border.*

Num 20:17 "Please let us pass through your land. We will not pass through field or through vineyard, neither will we drink from the water of the wells. We will go along the king's highway. We will not turn away to the right hand nor to the left, until we have passed your border."

Num 20:18 Edom said to him, "You shall not pass through me, lest I come out with the sword against you."

Num 20:19 The children of Israel said to him, "We will go up by the highway; and if we drink your water, I and my livestock, then I will give its price. Only let me, without doing anything else, pass through on my feet."

Num 20:20 He said, "You shall not pass through." Edom came out against him with many people, and with a strong hand.

MY NOTES

Num 20:21 Thus Edom refused to give Israel passage through his border, so Israel turned away from him.

The Death of Aaron

THURSDAY Num 20:22 They traveled from Kadesh: and the children of Israel, even the whole congregation, came to Mount Hor.

Num 20:23 YHWH spoke to Moses and Aaron in Mount Hor, by the border of the land of Edom, saying,

Num 20:24 "Aaron shall be gathered to his people; for he shall not enter into the land which I have given to the children of Israel, because you rebelled against my word at the waters of Meribah.

Num 20:25 Take Aaron and Eleazar his son, and bring them up to Mount Hor;

Num 20:26 and strip Aaron of his garments, and put them on Eleazar his son. Aaron shall be gathered, and shall die there."

Num 20:27 Moses did as YHWH commanded. They went up into Mount Hor in the sight of all the congregation.

Num 20:28 *Moses stripped Aaron of his garments, and put them on Eleazar his son. Aaron died there on the top of the mountain, and Moses and Eleazar came down from the mountain.*

Num 20:29 When all the congregation saw that Aaron was dead, they wept for Aaron thirty days, even all the house of Israel.

Arad Destroyed

Num 21:1 The Canaanite, the king of Arad, who lived in the South, heard that Israel came by the way of Atharim. He fought against Israel, and took some of them captive.

Num 21:2 Israel vowed a vow to YHWH, and said, "If you will indeed deliver this people into my hand, then I will utterly destroy their cities."

Num 21:3 YHWH listened to the voice of Israel, and delivered up the Canaanites; and they utterly destroyed them and their cities. The name of the place was called Hormah.

The Bronze Serpent

Num 21:4 They traveled from Mount Hor by the way to the Red Sea, to go around the land of Edom The soul of the people was very discouraged because of the journey.

Num 21:5 The people spoke against God, and against Moses, "Why have you brought us up out of Egypt to die in the wilderness? For there is no bread, and there is no water; and our soul loathes this disgusting bread."

MY NOTES

Num 21:6 YHWH sent venomous snakes among the people, and they bit the people. Many people of Israel died.

Num 21:7 The people came to Moses, and said, "We have sinned, because we have spoken against YHWH, and against you. Pray to YHWH, that he take away the serpents from us." Moses prayed for the people.

Num 21:8 YHWH said to Moses, "Make a venomous snake, and set it on a pole. It shall happen, that everyone who is bitten, when he sees it, shall live."

Num 21:9 **Moses made a serpent of brass, and set it on the pole. If a serpent had bitten any man, when he looked at the serpent of brass, he lived.**

The Song of the Well

FRIDAY Num 21:10 The children of Israel traveled, and encamped in Oboth.

Num 21:11 They traveled from Oboth, and encamped at Iyeabarim, in the wilderness which is before Moab, toward the sunrise.

Num 21:12 From there they traveled, and encamped in the valley of Zered.

Num 21:13 From there they traveled, and encamped on the other side of the Arnon, which is in the wilderness, that comes out of the border of the Amorites: for the Arnon is the border of Moab, between Moab and the Amorites.

Num 21:14 Therefore it is said in the book of the Wars of YHWH, "Vaheb in Suphah, the valleys of the Arnon,

Num 21:15 the slope of the valleys that incline toward the dwelling of Ar, leans on the border of Moab."

Num 21:16 From there they traveled to Beer; that is the well of which YHWH said to Moses, "Gather the people together, and I will give them water."

Num 21:17 **Then Israel sang this song: "Spring up, well! Sing to it,**

Num 21:18 **the well, which the princes dug, which the nobles of the people dug, with the scepter, and with their poles."** From the wilderness they traveled to Mattanah;

Num 21:19 and from Mattanah to Nahaliel; and from Nahaliel to Bamoth;

Num 21:20 and from Bamoth to the valley that is in the field of Moab, to the top of Pisgah, which looks down on the desert.

King Sihon Defeated

SABBATH Num 21:21 Israel sent messengers to Sihon king of the Amorites, saying,

MY NOTES

Num 21:22 "Let me pass through your land. We will not turn away into field or vineyard. We will not drink of the water of the wells. We will go by the king's highway, until we have passed your border."

Num 21:23 Sihon would not allow Israel to pass through his border, but Sihon gathered all his people together, and went out against Israel into the wilderness, and came to Jahaz. He fought against Israel.

Num 21:24 Israel struck him with the edge of the sword, and possessed his land from the Arnon to the Jabbok, even to the children of Ammon; for the border of the children of Ammon was strong.

Num 21:25 Israel took all these cities. Israel lived in all the cities of the Amorites, in Heshbon, and in all its villages.

Num 21:26 For Heshbon was the city of Sihon the king of the Amorites, who had fought against the former king of Moab, and taken all his land out of his hand, even to the Arnon.

Num 21:27 Therefore those who speak in proverbs say, "Come to Heshbon. Let the city of Sihon be built and established;

Num 21:28 for a fire has gone out of Heshbon, a flame from the city of Sihon. It has devoured Ar of Moab, The lords of the high places of the Arnon.

Num 21:29 Woe to you, Moab! You are undone, people of Chemosh! He has given his sons as fugitives, and his daughters into captivity, to Sihon king of the Amorites.

Num 21:30 We have shot at them. Heshbon has perished even to Dibon. We have laid waste even to Nophah, Which reaches to Medeba."

King Og Defeated

Num 21:31 Thus Israel lived in the land of the Amorites.

Num 21:32 Moses sent to spy out Jazer. They took its villages, and drove out the Amorites who were there.

Num 21:33 They turned and went up by the way of Bashan. Og the king of Bashan went out against them, he and all his people, to battle at Edrei.

Num 21:34 **YHWH said to Moses, "Don't fear him, for I have delivered him into your hand, with all his people, and his land. You shall do to him as you did to Sihon king of the Amorites, who lived at Heshbon."**

Num 21:35 So they struck him, with his sons and all his people, until there were no survivors; and they possessed his land.

Balak Summons Balaam

Num 22:1 The children of Israel traveled, and encamped in the plains of Moab beyond the Jordan at Jericho.

CHUKAT SCRAMBLE

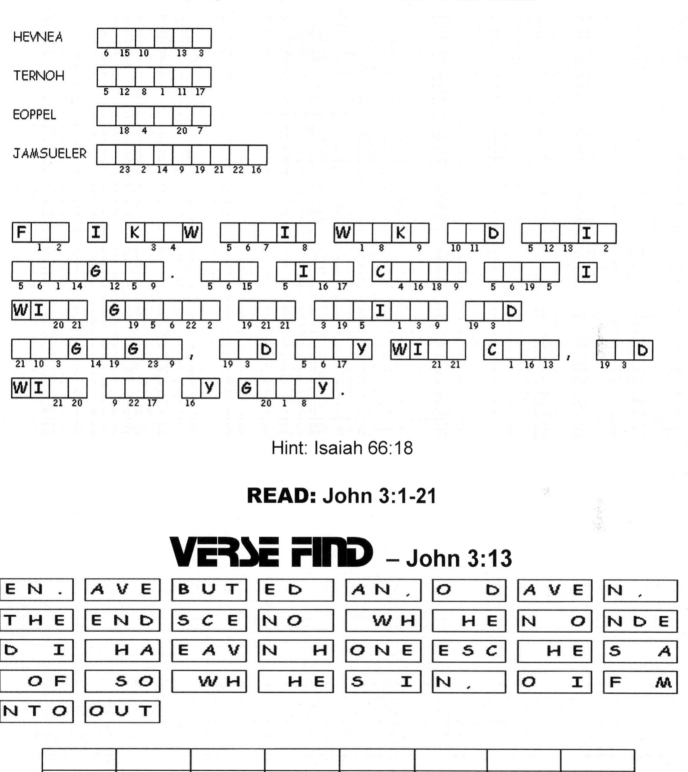

HEVNEA ⬜⬜⬜⬜⬜
6 15 10 13 3

TERNOH ⬜⬜⬜⬜⬜⬜
5 12 8 1 11 17

EOPPEL ⬜⬜⬜⬜⬜⬜
18 4 20 7

JAMSUELER ⬜⬜⬜⬜⬜⬜⬜⬜⬜
23 2 14 9 19 21 22 16

Hint: Isaiah 66:18

READ: John 3:1-21

VERSE FIND – John 3:13

EN .	AVE	BUT	ED	AN ,	O D	AVE	N .
THE	END	SCE	NO		WH	HE N	O NDE
D I	HA	EAV N H	ONE	ESC		HE	S A
OF	SO	WH	HE	S	IN ,	O I F M	
NTO	OUT						

BALAK

בָּלָק

NUMBERS

It Means: **BALAK, THE SON OF ZIPPOR, KING OF MOAB**

Our Fortieth Torah Portion is called Balak! בָּלָק
Numbers 22:2 – Numbers 25:9
PROPHETS: Micah 5:7-6:8
NEW TESTAMENT: Mark 11:12-26; Romans 11:25-32;1 Corinthians 1:20-31; Hebrews 1:1-2; 2 Peter 2:1-22; Jude 11; Revelation 2:12-17

MAKE A MARK
Each time you hear someone say one of the words below make a '**/**" beside the word. See how many marks you can get!

angel	
altar	
seven	
Balaam	
YHWH	
said	

FIRST FIND
~
If someone mentions a verse or scripture that is NOT in this Torah Portion, see if YOU can be the First to Find it!

This Weeks Torah Portion is:

Parsha: _____

Scriptures: _____

Name: _____

My Favorite Song was:

date: _____

I talked to _____ about Today's Study.

words I didn't Understand

?!

The Most IMPORTANT thing I Learned today was:

MY NOTES

Draw something you learned today

I brought My Bible with me ☐
✓ I am sitting with my Family ☐
I am ready to listen Carefully ☐

SUNDAY Num 22:2 Balak the son of Zippor saw all that Israel had done to the Amorites.

Num 22:3 Moab was very afraid of the people, because they were many. Moab was distressed because of the children of Israel.

Num 22:4 Moab said to the elders of Midian, "Now this multitude will lick up all that is around us, as the ox licks up the grass of the field." Balak the son of Zippor was king of Moab at that time.

Num 22:5 He sent messengers to Balaam the son of Beor, to Pethor, which is by the River, to the land of the children of his people, to call him, saying, "Behold, there is a people who came out of Egypt. Behold, they cover the surface of the earth, and they are staying opposite me.

Num 22:6 Please come now therefore curse me this people; for they are too mighty for me. Perhaps I shall prevail, that we may strike them, and that I may drive them out of the land; for I know that he whom you bless is blessed, and he whom you curse is cursed."

Num 22:7 The elders of Moab and the elders of Midian departed with the rewards of divination in their hand. They came to Balaam, and spoke to him the words of Balak.

Num 22:8 He said to them, "Lodge here this night, and I will bring you word again, as YHWH shall speak to me." The princes of Moab stayed with Balaam.

Num 22:9 God came to Balaam, and said, "Who are these men with you?"

Num 22:10 Balaam said to God, "Balak the son of Zippor, king of Moab, has said to me,

Num 22:11 'Behold, the people that has come out of Egypt covers the surface of the earth. Now, come curse me them. Perhaps I shall be able to fight against them, and shall drive them out.'"

Num 22:12 **God said to Balaam, "You shall not go with them. You shall not curse the people; for they are blessed."**

MONDAY Num 22:13 Balaam rose up in the morning, and said to the princes of Balak, "Go to your land; for YHWH refuses to permit me to go with you."

Num 22:14 The princes of Moab rose up, and they went to Balak, and said, "Balaam refuses to come with us."

Num 22:15 Balak again sent princes, more, and more honorable than they.

Num 22:16 They came to Balaam, and said to him, "Thus says Balak the son of Zippor, 'Please let nothing hinder you from coming to me,

MY NOTES

Num 22:17 for I will promote you to very great honor, and whatever you say to me I will do. Please come therefore, and curse this people for me.'"

Num 22:18 Balaam answered the servants of Balak, "If Balak would give me his house full of silver and gold, I can't go beyond the word of YHWH my God, to do less or more.

Num 22:19 Now therefore please stay here tonight as well, that I may know what else YHWH will speak to me."

Num 22:20 **God came to Balaam at night, and said to him, "If the men have come to call you, rise up, go with them; but only the word which I speak to you, that you shall do."**

<u>TUESDAY</u> Num 22:21 Balaam rose up in the morning, and saddled his donkey, and went with the princes of Moab.

Balaam's Donkey and the Angel

Num 22:22 God's anger burned because he went; and YHWH's angel placed himself in the way for an adversary against him. Now he was riding on his donkey, and his two servants were with him.

Num 22:23 The donkey saw YHWH's angel standing in the way, with his sword drawn in his hand; and the donkey turned out of the path, and went into the field. Balaam struck the donkey, to turn her into the path.

Num 22:24 Then YHWH's angel stood in a narrow path between the vineyards, a wall being on this side, and a wall on that side.

Num 22:25 The donkey saw YHWH's angel, and she thrust herself to the wall, and crushed Balaam's foot against the wall. He struck her again.

Num 22:26 YHWH's angel went further, and stood in a narrow place, where there was no way to turn either to the right hand or to the left.

Num 22:27 The donkey saw YHWH's angel, and she lay down under Balaam. Balaam's anger burned, and he struck the donkey with his staff.

Num 22:28 **YHWH opened the mouth of the donkey, and she said to Balaam, "What have I done to you, that you have struck me these three times?"**

Num 22:29 Balaam said to the donkey, "Because you have mocked me, I wish there were a sword in my hand, for now I would have killed you."

Num 22:30 The donkey said to Balaam, "Am I not your donkey, on which you have ridden all your life long until today? Was I ever in the habit of doing so to you?" He said, "No."

Num 22:31 Then YHWH opened the eyes of Balaam, and he saw YHWH's angel standing in the way, with his sword drawn in his hand; and he bowed his head, and fell on his face.

Num 22:32 YHWH's angel said to him, "Why have you struck your donkey these three times? Behold, I have come out as an adversary, because your way is perverse before me.

Num 22:33 The donkey saw me, and turned away before me these three times. Unless she had turned away from me, surely now I would have killed you, and saved her alive."

Num 22:34 Balaam said to YHWH's angel, "I have sinned; for I didn't know that you stood in the way against me. Now therefore, if it displeases you, I will go back again."

Num 22:35 YHWH's angel said to Balaam, "Go with the men; but only the word that I shall speak to you, that you shall speak." So Balaam went with the princes of Balak.

Num 22:36 When Balak heard that Balaam had come, he went out to meet him to the City of Moab, which is on the border of the Arnon, which is in the utmost part of the border.

Num 22:37 Balak said to Balaam, "Didn't I earnestly send for you to summon you? Why didn't you come to me? Am I not able indeed to promote you to honor?"

Num 22:38 Balaam said to Balak, "Behold, I have come to you. Have I now any power at all to speak anything? The word that God puts in my mouth, that shall I speak."

WEDNESDAY Num 22:39 Balaam went with Balak, and they came to Kiriath Huzoth.

Num 22:40 Balak sacrificed cattle and sheep, and sent to Balaam, and to the princes who were with him.

Num 22:41 In the morning, Balak took Balaam, and brought him up into the high places of Baal; and he saw from there part of the people.

Balaam's First Oracle

Num 23:1 Balaam said to Balak, "Build here seven altars for me, and prepare here seven bulls and seven rams for me."

Num 23:2 Balak did as Balaam had spoken; and Balak and Balaam offered on every altar a bull and a ram.

Num 23:3 Balaam said to Balak, "Stand by your burnt offering, and I will go. Perhaps YHWH will come to meet me. Whatever he shows me I will tell you." He went to a bare height.

Num 23:4 God met Balaam, and he said to him, "I have prepared the seven altars, and I have offered up a bull and a ram on every altar."

Num 23:5 YHWH put a word in Balaam's mouth, and said, "Return to Balak, and thus you shall speak."

Num 23:6 He returned to him, and behold, he was standing by his burnt offering, he, and all the princes of Moab.

Num 23:7 He took up his parable, and said, "From Aram has Balak brought me, the king of Moab from the mountains of the East. Come, curse Jacob for me. Come, defy Israel.

Num 23:8 *How shall I curse whom God has not cursed? How shall I defy whom YHWH has not defied?*

Num 23:9 For from the top of the rocks I see him. From the hills I see him. Behold, it is a people that dwells alone, and shall not be listed among the nations.

Num 23:10 Who can count the dust of Jacob, or count the fourth part of Israel? Let me die the death of the righteous! Let my last end be like his!"

Num 23:11 Balak said to Balaam, "What have you done to me? I took you to curse my enemies, and behold, you have blessed them altogether."

Num 23:12 He answered and said, "Must I not take heed to speak that which YHWH puts in my mouth?"

Balaam's Second Oracle

THURSDAY Num 23:13 Balak said to him, "Please come with me to another place, where you may see them. You shall see just part of them, and shall not see them all. Curse them from there for me."

Num 23:14 He took him into the field of Zophim, to the top of Pisgah, and built seven altars, and offered up a bull and a ram on every altar.

Num 23:15 He said to Balak, "Stand here by your burnt offering, while I meet God over there."

Num 23:16 YHWH met Balaam, and put a word in his mouth, and said, "Return to Balak, and say this."

Num 23:17 He came to him, and behold, he was standing by his burnt offering, and the princes of Moab with him. Balak said to him, "What has YHWH spoken?"

Num 23:18 He took up his parable, and said, "Rise up, Balak, and hear! Listen to me, you son of Zippor.

Num 23:19 *God is not a man, that he should lie, nor a son of man, that he should repent. Has he said, and will he not do it? Or has he spoken, and will he not make it good?*

Num 23:20 Behold, I have received a command to bless. He has blessed, and I can't reverse it.

Num 23:21 He has not seen iniquity in Jacob. Neither has he seen perverseness in Israel. YHWH his God is with him. The shout of a king is among them.

Num 23:22 God brings them out of Egypt. He has as it were the strength of the wild ox.

MY NOTES

Num 23:23 Surely there is no enchantment with Jacob; Neither is there any divination with Israel. Now it shall be said of Jacob and of Israel, 'What has God done!'

Num 23:24 Behold, the people rises up as a lioness. As a lion he lifts himself up. He shall not lie down until he eats of the prey, and drinks the blood of the slain."

Num 23:25 Balak said to Balaam, "Neither curse them at all, nor bless them at all."

Num 23:26 But Balaam answered Balak, "Didn't I tell you, saying, 'All that YHWH speaks, that I must do?'"

FRIDAY Num 23:27 Balak said to Balaam, "Come now, I will take you to another place; perhaps it will please God that you may curse them for me from there."

Num 23:28 Balak took Balaam to the top of Peor, that looks down on the desert.

Num 23:29 Balaam said to Balak, "Build seven altars for me here, and prepare seven bulls and seven rams for me here."

Num 23:30 Balak did as Balaam had said, and offered up a bull and a ram on every altar.

Balaam's Third Oracle

Num 24:1 When Balaam saw that it pleased YHWH to bless Israel, he didn't go, as at the other times, to meet with enchantments, but he set his face toward the wilderness.

Num 24:2 Balaam lifted up his eyes, and he saw Israel dwelling according to their tribes; and the Spirit of God came on him.

Num 24:3 He took up his parable, and said, "Balaam the son of Beor says, the man whose eyes are open says;

Num 24:4 he says, who hears the words of God, who sees the vision of the Almighty, falling down, and having his eyes open:

Num 24:5 How goodly are your tents, Jacob, and your tents, Israel!

Num 24:6 As valleys they are spread out, as gardens by the riverside, as aloes which YHWH has planted, as cedar trees beside the waters.

Num 24:7 Water shall flow from his buckets. His seed shall be in many waters. His king shall be higher than Agag. His kingdom shall be exalted.

Num 24:8 God brings him out of Egypt. He has as it were the strength of the wild ox. He shall eat up the nations his adversaries, shall break their bones in pieces, and pierce them with his arrows.

Num 24:9 *He couched, he lay down as a lion, as a lioness; who shall rouse him up? Everyone who blesses you is blessed. Everyone who curses you is cursed."*

MY NOTES

_____
_____
_____
_____
_____
_____
_____
_____
_____
_____
_____
_____
_____
_____
_____
_____
_____
_____
_____
_____
_____
_____
_____
_____
_____
_____
_____

Num 24:10 Balak's anger burned against Balaam, and he struck his hands together. Balak said to Balaam, "I called you to curse my enemies, and, behold, you have altogether blessed them these three times.

Num 24:11 Therefore, flee to your place, now! I thought to promote you to great honor; but, behold, YHWH has kept you back from honor."

Num 24:12 Balaam said to Balak, "Didn't I also tell your messengers whom you sent to me, saying,

Num 24:13 'If Balak would give me his house full of silver and gold, I can't go beyond YHWH's word, to do either good or bad from my own mind. I will say what YHWH says'?

Num 24:14 Now, behold, I go to my people. Come, I will inform you what this people shall do to your people in the latter days."

Balaam's Final Oracle

SABBATH Num 24:15 He took up his parable, and said, "Balaam the son of Beor says, the man whose eyes are open says;

Num 24:16 he says, who hears the words of God, knows the knowledge of the Most High, and who sees the vision of the Almighty, Falling down, and having his eyes open:

Num 24:17 I see him, but not now. I see him, but not near. A star will come out of Jacob. A scepter will rise out of Israel, and shall strike through the corners of Moab, and break down all the sons of Sheth.

Num 24:18 Edom shall be a possession. Seir, his enemies, also shall be a possession, while Israel does valiantly.

Num 24:19 Out of Jacob shall one have dominion, and shall destroy the remnant from the city."

Num 24:20 He looked at Amalek, and took up his parable, and said, "Amalek was the first of the nations, But his latter end shall come to destruction."

Num 24:21 He looked at the Kenite, and took up his parable, and said, "Your dwelling place is strong. Your nest is set in the rock.

Num 24:22 Nevertheless Kain shall be wasted, until Asshur carries you away captive."

Num 24:23 He took up his parable, and said, "Alas, who shall live when God does this?

Num 24:24 But ships shall come from the coast of Kittim. They shall afflict Asshur, and shall afflict Eber. He also shall come to destruction."

Num 24:25 Balaam rose up, and went and returned to his place; and Balak also went his way.

Baal Worship at Peor

Num 25:1 Israel stayed in Shittim; and the people began to play the prostitute with the daughters of Moab;

Num 25:2 for they called the people to the sacrifices of their gods. The people ate and bowed down to their gods.

Num 25:3 Israel joined himself to Baal Peor. YHWH's anger burned against Israel.

Num 25:4 YHWH said to Moses, "Take all the chiefs of the people, and hang them up to YHWH before the sun, that the fierce anger of YHWH may turn away from Israel."

Num 25:5 Moses said to the judges of Israel, "Everyone kill his men who have joined themselves to Baal Peor."

Num 25:6 Behold, one of the children of Israel came and brought to his brothers a Midianite woman in the sight of Moses, and in the sight of all the congregation of the children of Israel, while they were weeping at the door of the Tent of Meeting.

Num 25:7 When Phinehas, the son of Eleazar, the son of Aaron the priest, saw it, he rose up from the middle of the congregation, and took a spear in his hand.

Num 25:8 He went after the man of Israel into the pavilion, and thrust both of them through, the man of Israel, and the woman through her body. So the plague was stayed from the children of Israel.

Num 25:9 Those who died by the plague were twenty-four thousand.

CRYPTOGRAM – MICAH 6:4

A	B	C	D	E	F	G	H	I	J	K	L	M	N	O	P	Q	R	S	T	U	V	W	X	Y	Z
								16					8	13			25		1						

```
    _  O  R    I      _  R  O  _  _  _  T    _  O  _    _  _    O  T  O
   26 13 25   16     18 25 13 14  5 20  1    2 13 14   14 10   13 14  1   13 26

T  _  _  _    _  N  _  O    _  _  _  _  _     T  _  N  _    R  _  _  _  _  _  _  _
1 20 17   12 24  8  6   13 26   17  5  2 10  1   ,   24  8  6    25 17  6 17 17  3 17  6

   _  O    _  O  T  O    _  T  O    _  _  _  _  _    O  _    _  O  N  _  _  _
   2 13 14   13 14  1   13 26    1 20 17   20 13 14  7 17   13 26   18 13  8  6 24  5

   _ . I    _  N  T  _    _  _  O  R  _    _  O  _    _  O  _  _  _  ,
  17  16    7 17  8  1   18 17 26 13 25 17    2 13 14   3 13  7 17  7

          _  _  R  O  N  ,  _  N  _    _  I  R  I  _  _  .
         24 24 25 13  8    24  8  6    3 16 25 16 24  3
```

VERSE FIND – MARK 11:26

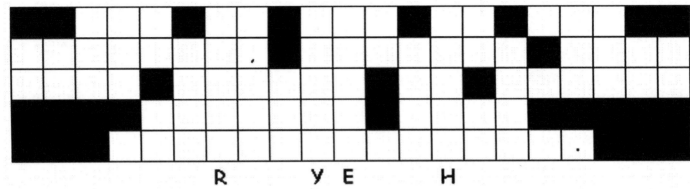

```
              R       Y E       H
         T F V E F   R O   T N E N
       U G T F N G G V E S Y D O R S A T
 F O R R R A A T H E R U I O U H N O I L L
 Y O B U I O I S I N E I S I O R E W V E N
```

HELP DONKEY GET TO MOAB

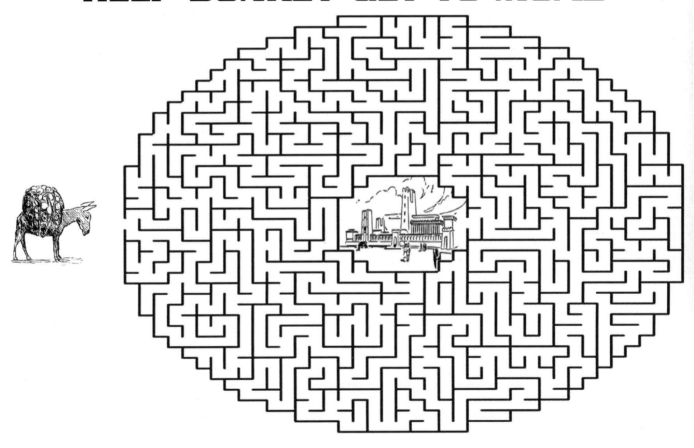

PINECHAS

פִּינְחָס

NUMBERS

It Means: PHINEHAS

Our Forty-first Torah Portion is called Pinechas! פִּינְחָס
Numbers 25:10 – Numbers 30:1
PROPHETS: 1 Kings 18:46-19:21;
NEW TESTAMENT: Matthew 26:1-30; John 2:13-25; 7:1-39; 11:55-12:1; 13:1; 18:28, 39; 19:14;
Acts 2:1-21; 12:3-4; 20:6-16; 27:9-11; 1 Corinthians 5:6-8; 16:8; Hebrews 11:28

MAKE A MARK

Each time you hear someone say one of the words below make a '/" beside the word. See how many marks you can get!

Joshua	
people	
Sukkot	
land	
sons	
climb	

FIRST FIND

~

If someone mentions a verse or scripture that is NOT in this Torah Portion, see if YOU can be the First to Find it!

This Weeks Torah Portion is:

Parsha: _____

Scriptures: _____

Name:_____

words I didn't Understand

?!

My Favorite Song was:

date: _____

The Most IMPORTANT thing I Learned today was:

I talked to _____
about Today's Study.

MY NOTES

Draw something you learned today

✓ I brought My Bible with me
I am sitting with my Family
I am ready to listen Carefully

The Zeal of Phinehas

SUNDAY Num 25:10 YHWH spoke to Moses, saying,

Num 25:11 "Phinehas, the son of Eleazar, the son of Aaron the priest, has turned my wrath away from the children of Israel, in that he was jealous with my jealousy among them, so that I didn't consume the children of Israel in my jealousy.

Num 25:12 Therefore say, 'Behold, I give to him my covenant of peace.

Num 25:13 It shall be to him, and to his offspring after him, the covenant of an everlasting priesthood, because he was jealous for his God, and made atonement for the children of Israel.'"

Num 25:14 Now the name of the man of Israel that was slain, who was slain with the Midianite woman, was Zimri, the son of Salu, a prince of a fathers' house among the Simeonites.

Num 25:15 The name of the Midianite woman who was slain was Cozbi, the daughter of Zur. He was head of the people of a fathers' house in Midian.

Num 25:16 YHWH spoke to Moses, saying,

Num 25:17 "Harass the Midianites, and strike them,

Num 25:18 for they harassed you with their wiles, wherein they have deceived you in the matter of Peor, and in the incident regarding Cozbi, the daughter of the prince of Midian, their sister, who was slain on the day of the plague in the matter of Peor."

Census of the New Generation

Num 26:1 After the plague, YHWH spoke to Moses and to Eleazar the son of Aaron the priest, saying,

Num 26:2 *"Take a census of all the congregation of the children of Israel, from twenty years old and upward, by their fathers' houses, all who are able to go out to war in Israel."*

Num 26:3 Moses and Eleazar the priest spoke with them in the plains of Moab by the Jordan at Jericho, saying,

Num 26:4 "Take a census, from twenty years old and upward; as YHWH commanded Moses and the children of Israel." These are those that came out of the land of Egypt.

MONDAY Num 26:5 Reuben, the firstborn of Israel; the sons of Reuben: of Hanoch, the family of the Hanochites; of Pallu, the family of the Palluites;

Num 26:6 of Hezron, the family of the Hezronites; of Carmi, the family of the Carmites.

Num 26:7 These are the families of the Reubenites; and those who were counted of them were forty-three thousand seven hundred thirty.

Num 26:8 The sons of Pallu: Eliab.

Num 26:9 The sons of Eliab: Nemuel, and Dathan, and Abiram. These are that Dathan and Abiram, who were called by the congregation, who rebelled against Moses and against Aaron in the company of Korah, when they rebelled against YHWH,

Num 26:10 and the earth opened its mouth, and swallowed them up together with Korah, when that company died; at the time the fire devoured two hundred fifty men, and they became a sign.

Num 26:11 Notwithstanding, the sons of Korah didn't die.

Num 26:12 The sons of Simeon after their families: of Nemuel, the family of the Nemuelites; of Jamin, the family of the Jaminites; of Jachin, the family of the Jachinites;

Num 26:13 of Zerah, the family of the Zerahites; of Shaul, the family of the Shaulites.

Num 26:14 These are the families of the Simeonites, twenty-two thousand two hundred.

Num 26:15 The sons of Gad after their families: of Zephon, the family of the Zephonites; of Haggi, the family of the Haggites; of Shuni, the family of the Shunites;

Num 26:16 of Ozni, the family of the Oznites; of Eri, the family of the Erites;

Num 26:17 of Arod, the family of the Arodites; of Areli, the family of the Arelites.

Num 26:18 These are the families of the sons of Gad according to those who were counted of them, forty thousand and five hundred.

Num 26:19 The sons of Judah: Er and Onan. Er and Onan died in the land of Canaan.

Num 26:20 The sons of Judah after their families were: of Shelah, the family of the Shelanites; of Perez, the family of the Perezites; of Zerah, the family of the Zerahites.

Num 26:21 The sons of Perez were: of Hezron, the family of the Hezronites; of Hamul, the family of the Hamulites.

Num 26:22 These are the families of Judah according to those who were counted of them, seventy-six thousand five hundred.

Num 26:23 The sons of Issachar after their families: of Tola, the family of the Tolaites; of Puvah, the family of the Punites;

Num 26:24 of Jashub, the family of the Jashubites; of Shimron, the family of the Shimronites.

Num 26:25 These are the families of Issachar according to those who were counted of them, sixty-four thousand three hundred.

Num 26:26 The sons of Zebulun after their families: of Sered, the family of the Seredites; of Elon, the family of the Elonites; of Jahleel, the family of the Jahleelites.

MY NOTES

Num 26:27 These are the families of the Zebulunites according to those who were counted of them, sixty thousand five hundred.

Num 26:28 The sons of Joseph after their families: Manasseh and Ephraim.

Num 26:29 The sons of Manasseh: of Machir, the family of the Machirites; and Machir became the father of Gilead; of Gilead, the family of the Gileadites.

Num 26:30 These are the sons of Gilead: of Iezer, the family of the Iezerites; of Helek, the family of the Helekites;

Num 26:31 and Asriel, the family of the Asrielites; and Shechem, the family of the Shechemites;

Num 26:32 and Shemida, the family of the Shemidaites; and Hepher, the family of the Hepherites.

Num 26:33 Zelophehad the son of Hepher had no sons, but daughters: and the names of the daughters of Zelophehad were Mahlah, and Noah, Hoglah, Milcah, and Tirzah.

Num 26:34 These are the families of Manasseh. Those who were counted of them were fifty-two thousand seven hundred.

Num 26:35 These are the sons of Ephraim after their families: of Shuthelah, the family of the Shuthelahites; of Becher, the family of the Becherites; of Tahan, the family of the Tahanites.

Num 26:36 These are the sons of Shuthelah: of Eran, the family of the Eranites.

Num 26:37 These are the families of the sons of Ephraim according to those who were counted of them, thirty-two thousand five hundred. These are the sons of Joseph after their families.

Num 26:38 The sons of Benjamin after their families: of Bela, the family of the Belaites; of Ashbel, the family of the Ashbelites; of Ahiram, the family of the Ahiramites;

Num 26:39 of Shephupham, the family of the Shuphamites; of Hupham, the family of the Huphamites.

Num 26:40 The sons of Bela were Ard and Naaman: the family of the Ardites; of Naaman, the family of the Naamites.

Num 26:41 These are the sons of Benjamin after their families; and those who were counted of them were forty-five thousand six hundred.

Num 26:42 These are the sons of Dan after their families: of Shuham, the family of the Shuhamites. These are the families of Dan after their families.

Num 26:43 All the families of the Shuhamites, according to those who were counted of them, were sixty-four thousand four hundred.

Num 26:44 The sons of Asher after their families: of Imnah, the family of the Imnites; of Ishvi, the family of the Ishvites; of Beriah, the family of the Berites.

Num 26:45 Of the sons of Beriah: of Heber, the family of the Heberites; of Malchiel, the family of the Malchielites.

Num 26:46 The name of the daughter of Asher was Serah.

Num 26:47 These are the families of the sons of Asher according to those who were counted of them, fifty-three thousand and four hundred.

Num 26:48 The sons of Naphtali after their families: of Jahzeel, the family of the Jahzeelites; of Guni, the family of the Gunites;

Num 26:49 of Jezer, the family of the Jezerites; of Shillem, the family of the Shillemites.

Num 26:50 These are the families of Naphtali according to their families; and those who were counted of them were forty-five thousand four hundred.

Num 26:51 These are those who were counted of the children of Israel, six hundred one thousand seven hundred thirty.

TUESDAY Num 26:52 YHWH spoke to Moses, saying,

Num 26:53 "To these the land shall be divided for an inheritance according to the number of names.

Num 26:54 To the more you shall give the more inheritance, and to the fewer you shall give the less inheritance. To everyone according to those who were counted of him shall his inheritance be given.

Num 26:55 Notwithstanding, the land shall be divided by lot. According to the names of the tribes of their fathers they shall inherit.

Num 26:56 According to the lot shall their inheritance be divided between the more and the fewer."

Num 26:57 These are those who were counted of the Levites after their families: of Gershon, the family of the Gershonites; of Kohath, the family of the Kohathites; of Merari, the family of the Merarites.

Num 26:58 These are the families of Levi: the family of the Libnites, the family of the Hebronites, the family of the Mahlites, the family of the Mushites, the family of the Korahites. Kohath became the father of Amram.

Num 26:59 The name of Amram's wife was Jochebed, the daughter of Levi, who was born to Levi in Egypt. She bore to Amram Aaron and Moses, and Miriam their sister.

Num 26:60 To Aaron were born Nadab and Abihu, Eleazar and Ithamar.

Num 26:61 Nadab and Abihu died when they offered strange fire before YHWH.

MY NOTES

Num 26:62 Those who were counted of them were twenty-three thousand, every male from a month old and upward; for they were not counted among the children of Israel, because there was no inheritance given them among the children of Israel.

Num 26:63 These are those who were counted by Moses and Eleazar the priest, who counted the children of Israel in the plains of Moab by the Jordan at Jericho.

Num 26:64 *But among these there was not a man of them who were counted by Moses and Aaron the priest, who counted the children of Israel in the wilderness of Sinai.*

Num 26:65 For YHWH had said of them, "They shall surely die in the wilderness." There was not a man left of them, except Caleb the son of Jephunneh, and Joshua the son of Nun.

The Daughters of Zelophehad

Num 27:1 Then the daughters of Zelophehad, the son of Hepher, the son of Gilead, the son of Machir, the son of Manasseh, of the families of Manasseh the son of Joseph came near. These are the names of his daughters: Mahlah, Noah, and Hoglah, and Milcah, and Tirzah.

Num 27:2 They stood before Moses, and before Eleazar the priest, and before the princes and all the congregation, at the door of the Tent of Meeting, saying,

Num 27:3 "Our father died in the wilderness. He was not among the company of those who gathered themselves together against YHWH in the company of Korah, but he died in his own sin. He had no sons.

Num 27:4 Why should the name of our father be taken away from among his family, because he had no son? Give to us a possession among the brothers of our father."

Num 27:5 Moses brought their cause before YHWH.

WEDNESDAY Num 27:6 YHWH spoke to Moses, saying,

Num 27:7 "The daughters of Zelophehad speak right. You shall surely give them a possession of an inheritance among their father's brothers. You shall cause the inheritance of their father to pass to them.

Num 27:8 You shall speak to the children of Israel, saying, 'If a man dies, and has no son, then you shall cause his inheritance to pass to his daughter.

Num 27:9 If he has no daughter, then you shall give his inheritance to his brothers.

Num 27:10 If he has no brothers, then you shall give his inheritance to his father's brothers.

MY NOTES

Num 27:11 If his father has no brothers, then you shall give his inheritance to his kinsman who is next to him of his family, and he shall possess it. This shall be a statute and ordinance for the children of Israel, as YHWH commanded Moses.'"

Joshua to Succeed Moses

Num 27:12 YHWH said to Moses, "Go up into this mountain of Abarim, and see the land which I have given to the children of Israel.

Num 27:13 When you have seen it, you also shall be gathered to your people, as Aaron your brother was gathered;

Num 27:14 because in the strife of the congregation, you rebelled against my word in the wilderness of Zin, to honor me as holy at the waters before their eyes." (These are the waters of Meribah of Kadesh in the wilderness of Zin.)

Num 27:15 Moses spoke to YHWH, saying,

Num 27:16 "Let YHWH, the God of the spirits of all flesh, appoint a man over the congregation,

Num 27:17 who may go out before them, and who may come in before them, and who may lead them out, and who may bring them in; that the congregation of YHWH may not be as sheep which have no shepherd."

Num 27:18 **YHWH said to Moses, "Take Joshua the son of Nun, a man in whom is the Spirit, and lay your hand on him.**

Num 27:19 Set him before Eleazar the priest, and before all the congregation; and commission him in their sight.

Num 27:20 You shall give authority to him, that all the congregation of the children of Israel may obey.

Num 27:21 He shall stand before Eleazar the priest, who shall inquire for him by the judgment of the Urim before YHWH. At his word they shall go out, and at his word they shall come in, both he, and all the children of Israel with him, even all the congregation."

Num 27:22 Moses did as YHWH commanded him. He took Joshua, and set him before Eleazar the priest, and before all the congregation.

Num 27:23 He laid his hands on him, and commissioned him, as YHWH spoke by Moses.

Daily Offerings

THURSDAY Num 28:1 YHWH spoke to Moses, saying,

Num 28:2 **"Command the children of Israel, and tell them, 'See that you present my offering, my food for my offerings made by fire, of a pleasant aroma to me, in their due season.'**

MY NOTES

Num 28:3 You shall tell them, 'This is the offering made by fire which you shall offer to YHWH: male lambs a year old without defect, two day by day, for a continual burnt offering.

Num 28:4 You shall offer the one lamb in the morning, and you shall offer the other lamb at evening;

Num 28:5 with one tenth of an ephah of fine flour for a meal offering, mixed with the fourth part of a hin of beaten oil.

Num 28:6 It is a continual burnt offering, which was ordained in Mount Sinai for a pleasant aroma, an offering made by fire to YHWH.

Num 28:7 Its drink offering shall be the fourth part of a hin for the one lamb. You shall pour out a drink offering of strong drink to YHWH in the holy place.

Num 28:8 The other lamb you shall offer at evening. As the meal offering of the morning, and as its drink offering, you shall offer it, an offering made by fire, for a pleasant aroma to YHWH.

Sabbath Offerings

Num 28:9 "'On the Sabbath day, you shall offer two male lambs a year old without defect, and two tenths of an ephah of fine flour for a meal offering, mixed with oil, and its drink offering:

Num 28:10 this is the burnt offering of every Sabbath, in addition to the continual burnt offering, and its drink offering.

Monthly Offerings

Num 28:11 "'In the beginnings of your months, you shall offer a burnt offering to YHWH: two young bulls, and one ram, seven male lambs a year old without defect;

Num 28:12 and three tenths of an ephah of fine flour for a meal offering, mixed with oil, for each bull; and two tenth parts of fine flour for a meal offering, mixed with oil, for the one ram;

Num 28:13 and one tenth part of fine flour mixed with oil for a meal offering to every lamb; for a burnt offering of a pleasant aroma, an offering made by fire to YHWH.

Num 28:14 Their drink offerings shall be half a hin of wine for a bull, and the third part of a hin for the ram, and the fourth part of a hin for a lamb. This is the burnt offering of every month throughout the months of the year.

Num 28:15 One male goat for a sin offering to YHWH; it shall be offered in addition to the continual burnt offering, and its drink offering.

Passover Offerings

FRIDAY Num 28:16 *"'In the first month, on the fourteenth day of the month, is YHWH's Passover.*

Num 28:17 *On the fifteenth day of this month shall be a feast. Unleavened bread shall be eaten for seven days.*

MY NOTES

Num 28:18 In the first day shall be a holy convocation. You shall do no regular work;

Num 28:19 but you shall offer an offering made by fire, a burnt offering to YHWH: two young bulls, and one ram, and seven male lambs a year old; they shall be to you without defect;

Num 28:20 and their meal offering, fine flour mixed with oil. You shall offer three tenths for a bull, and two tenths for the ram.

Num 28:21 You shall offer one tenth for every lamb of the seven lambs;

Num 28:22 and one male goat for a sin offering, to make atonement for you.

Num 28:23 You shall offer these in addition to the burnt offering of the morning, which is for a continual burnt offering.

Num 28:24 In this way you shall offer daily, for seven days, the food of the offering made by fire, of a pleasant aroma to YHWH. It shall be offered in addition to the continual burnt offering, and its drink offering.

Num 28:25 On the seventh day you shall have a holy convocation. You shall do no regular work.

Offerings for the Feast of Weeks

Num 28:26 *"'Also in the day of the first fruits, when you offer a new meal offering to YHWH in your feast of weeks, you shall have a holy convocation. You shall do no regular work;*

Num 28:27 but you shall offer a burnt offering for a pleasant aroma to YHWH: two young bulls, one ram, seven male lambs a year old;

Num 28:28 and their meal offering, fine flour mixed with oil, three tenths for each bull, two tenths for the one ram,

Num 28:29 one tenth for every lamb of the seven lambs;

Num 28:30 one male goat, to make atonement for you.

Num 28:31 Besides the continual burnt offering, and its meal offering, you shall offer them and their drink offerings. See that they are without defect.

Offerings for the Feast of Trumpets

Num 29:1 *"'In the seventh month, on the first day of the month, you shall have a holy convocation; you shall do no regular work: it is a day of blowing of trumpets to you.*

Num 29:2 You shall offer a burnt offering for a pleasant aroma to YHWH: one young bull, one ram, seven male lambs a year old without defect;

Num 29:3 and their meal offering, fine flour mixed with oil, three tenths for the bull, two tenths for the ram,

Num 29:4 and one tenth for every lamb of the seven lambs;

MY NOTES

Num 29:5 and one male goat for a sin offering, to make atonement for you;

Num 29:6 in addition to the burnt offering of the new moon, and its meal offering, and the continual burnt offering and its meal offering, and their drink offerings, according to their ordinance, for a pleasant aroma, an offering made by fire to YHWH.

Offerings for the Day of Atonement

Num 29:7 *'"On the tenth day of this seventh month you shall have a holy convocation. You shall afflict your souls. You shall do no kind of work;*

Num 29:8 but you shall offer a burnt offering to YHWH for a pleasant aroma: one young bull, one ram, seven male lambs a year old; all without defect;

Num 29:9 and their meal offering, fine flour mixed with oil, three tenths for the bull, two tenths for the one ram,

Num 29:10 one tenth for every lamb of the seven lambs:

Num 29:11 one male goat for a sin offering; in addition to the sin offering of atonement, and the continual burnt offering, and its meal offering, and their drink offerings.

Offerings for the Feast of Booths

SABBATH Num 29:12 *'"On the fifteenth day of the seventh month you shall have a holy convocation. You shall do no regular work. You shall keep a feast to YHWH seven days.*

Num 29:13 You shall offer a burnt offering, an offering made by fire, of a pleasant aroma to YHWH: thirteen young bulls, two rams, fourteen male lambs a year old; all without defect;

Num 29:14 and their meal offering, fine flour mixed with oil, three tenths for every bull of the thirteen bulls, two tenths for each ram of the two rams,

Num 29:15 and one tenth for every lamb of the fourteen lambs;

Num 29:16 and one male goat for a sin offering, in addition to the continual burnt offering, its meal offering, and its drink offering.

Num 29:17 "On the second day you shall offer twelve young bulls, two rams, fourteen male lambs a year old without defect;

Num 29:18 and their meal offering and their drink offerings for the bulls, for the rams, and for the lambs, according to their number, after the ordinance;

Num 29:19 and one male goat for a sin offering; in addition to the continual burnt offering, with its meal offering and their drink offerings.

Num 29:20 "On the third day eleven bulls, two rams, fourteen male lambs a year old without defect;

Num 29:21 and their meal offering and their drink offerings for the bulls, for the rams, and for the lambs, according to their number, after the ordinance;

Num 29:22 and one male goat for a sin offering; in addition to the continual burnt offering, and its meal offering, and its drink offering.

Num 29:23 "'On the fourth day ten bulls, two rams, fourteen male lambs a year old without defect;

Num 29:24 their meal offering and their drink offerings for the bulls, for the rams, and for the lambs, according to their number, after the ordinance;

Num 29:25 and one male goat for a sin offering; in addition to the continual burnt offering, its meal offering, and its drink offering.

Num 29:26 "'On the fifth day nine bulls, two rams, fourteen male lambs a year old without defect;

Num 29:27 and their meal offering and their drink offerings for the bulls, for the rams, and for the lambs, according to their number, after the ordinance;

Num 29:28 and one male goat for a sin offering, in addition to the continual burnt offering, and its meal offering, and its drink offering.

Num 29:29 "'On the sixth day eight bulls, two rams, fourteen male lambs a year old without defect;

Num 29:30 and their meal offering and their drink offerings for the bulls, for the rams, and for the lambs, according to their number, after the ordinance;

Num 29:31 and one male goat for a sin offering; in addition to the continual burnt offering, its meal offering, and the drink offerings of it.

Num 29:32 "'On the seventh day seven bulls, two rams, fourteen male lambs a year old without defect;

Num 29:33 and their meal offering and their drink offerings for the bulls, for the rams, and for the lambs, according to their number, after the ordinance;

Num 29:34 and one male goat for a sin offering; in addition to the continual burnt offering, its meal offering, and its drink offering.

Num 29:35 ***"'On the eighth day you shall have a solemn assembly: you shall do no regular work;***

Num 29:36 but you shall offer a burnt offering, an offering made by fire, a pleasant aroma to YHWH: one bull, one ram, seven male lambs a year old without defect;

MY NOTES

Num 29:37 their meal offering and their drink offerings for the bull, for the ram, and for the lambs, shall be according to their number, after the ordinance:

Num 29:38 and one male goat for a sin offering, in addition to the continual burnt offering, with its meal offering, and its drink offering.

Num 29:39 "'You shall offer these to YHWH in your set feasts, in addition to your vows and your freewill offerings, for your burnt offerings, your meal offerings, your drink offerings, and your peace offerings.'"

Num 29:40 Moses told the children of Israel according to all that YHWH commanded Moses.

Men and Vows

Num 30:1 Moses spoke to the heads of the tribes of the children of Israel, saying, "This is the thing which YHWH has commanded.

PINECHAS WORD-FIND

```
A T O N E M E N T P F F Y A M
C E O S K J Y S R A Y B U I O
E S W F E V O N M S Q H I M S
H O J S F C Y K K S S Y O X E
V E H N E E H T V O J L B G S
I X X T C T R A J V R I Y D K
D D N A A U I I V E M A L A L
Y E L U M B U N N R E D H H E
P E B P K G B B A G E J T E S
B C E N S U S A O I S Z N H H
R T S K E E W G S O D C O P E
S E L C A N R E B A T I M O Q
W G Y U G R A P R Z Q H M L J
S A H E N I H P V K F N S E B
A J Z Y R X G U O E B U N Z Q
```

ATONEMENT
BOOTHS
CALEB
CENSUS
DAILY
JOSHUA
MIDIANITES

MONTHLY
MOSES
OFFERINGS
PASSOVER
PENTECOST

PHINEHAS
SABBATH
TABERNACLES
TRUMPETS
VOWS
WEEKS
ZELOPHEHAD

VERSE FIND – JOHN 19:14

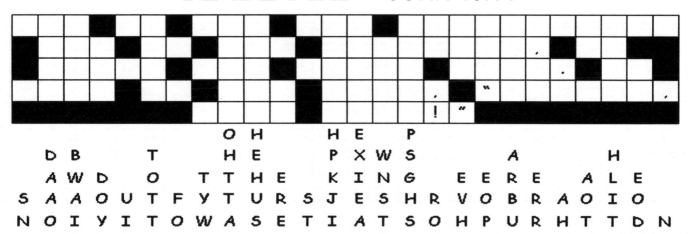

MATOT

מַטּוֹת

NUMBERS

It Means: **TRIBES**

Our Forty-Second Torah Portion is called Matot! מטות
Numbers 30:2 – Numbers 32:42
PROPHETS: Jeremiah 1 - 2:28; Judges 11:29-40
NEW TESTAMENT: Matthew 5:33-37; 23:1-39

MAKE A MARK
Each time you hear someone say one of the words below make a '**/**" beside the word. See how many marks you can get!

vow	
jealous	
husband	
corpse	
offering	
Jordan	

FIRST FIND

~

If someone mentions a verse or scripture that is NOT in this Torah Portion, see if YOU can be the First to Find it!

This Weeks Torah Portion is:

Parsha: _____

Scriptures: _____

Name: _____

My Favorite Song was:
_____

words I didn't Understand

?!

date:

I talked to _____
about Today's Study.

The Most IMPORTANT
thing I Learned today was:

MY NOTES

Draw something you learned today

I brought My Bible with me ☐
☑ I am sitting with my Family ☐
I am ready to listen Carefully ☐

SUNDAY Num 30:2 *When a man vows a vow to YHWH, or swears an oath to bind his soul with a bond, he shall not break his word. He shall do according to all that proceeds out of his mouth.*

Women and Vows

Num 30:3 "Also when a woman vows a vow to YHWH, and binds herself by a bond, being in her father's house, in her youth,

Num 30:4 and her father hears her vow, and her bond with which she has bound her soul, and her father says nothing to her; then all her vows shall stand, and every bond with which she has bound her soul shall stand.

Num 30:5 But if her father forbids her in the day that he hears, none of her vows, or of her bonds with which she has bound her soul, shall stand. YHWH will forgive her, because her father has forbidden her.

Num 30:6 "If she has a husband, while her vows are on her, or the rash utterance of her lips, with which she has bound her soul,

Num 30:7 and her husband hears it, and says nothing to her in the day that he hears it; then her vows shall stand, and her bonds with which she has bound her soul shall stand.

Num 30:8 But if her husband forbids her in the day that he hears it, then he shall make void her vow which is on her, and the rash utterance of her lips, with which she has bound her soul. YHWH will forgive her.

Num 30:9 "But the vow of a widow, or of her who is divorced, everything with which she has bound her soul, shall stand against her.

Num 30:10 "If she vowed in her husband's house, or bound her soul by a bond with an oath,

Num 30:11 and her husband heard it, and held his peace at her, and didn't disallow her; then all her vows shall stand, and every bond with which she bound her soul shall stand.

Num 30:12 But if her husband made them null and void in the day that he heard them, then whatever proceeded out of her lips concerning her vows, or concerning the bond of her soul, shall not stand. Her husband has made them void. YHWH will forgive her.

Num 30:13 Every vow, and every binding oath to afflict the soul, her husband may establish it, or her husband may make it void.

Num 30:14 But if her husband altogether says nothing to her from day to day, then he establishes all her vows, or all her bonds, which are on her. He has established them, because he said nothing to her in the day that he heard them.

MY NOTES

Num 30:15 But if he makes them null and void after he has heard them, then he shall bear her iniquity."

Num 30:16 These are the statutes which YHWH commanded Moses, between a man and his wife, between a father and his daughter, being in her youth, in her father's house.

Vengeance on Midian

MONDAY Num 31:1 YHWH spoke to Moses, saying,

Num 31:2 *"Avenge the children of Israel on the Midianites. Afterward you shall be gathered to your people."*

Num 31:3 Moses spoke to the people, saying, "Arm men from among you for war, that they may go against Midian, to execute YHWH's vengeance on Midian.

Num 31:4 Of every tribe one thousand, throughout all the tribes of Israel, you shall send to the war."

Num 31:5 So there were delivered, out of the thousands of Israel, a thousand of every tribe, twelve thousand armed for war.

Num 31:6 Moses sent them, one thousand of every tribe, to the war, them and Phinehas the son of Eleazar the priest, to the war, with the vessels of the sanctuary and the trumpets for the alarm in his hand.

Num 31:7 They fought against Midian, as YHWH commanded Moses. They killed every male.

Num 31:8 They killed the kings of Midian with the rest of their slain: Evi, Rekem, Zur, Hur, and Reba, the five kings of Midian. They also killed Balaam the son of Beor with the sword.

Num 31:9 The children of Israel took the women of Midian captive with their little ones; and all their livestock, all their flocks, and all their goods, they took as plunder.

Num 31:10 All their cities in the places in which they lived, and all their encampments, they burned with fire.

Num 31:11 They took all the captives, and all the plunder, both of man and of animal.

Num 31:12 They brought the captives, and the prey, and the plunder, to Moses, and to Eleazar the priest, and to the congregation of the children of Israel, to the camp at the plains of Moab, which are by the Jordan at Jericho.

TUESDAY Num 31:13 Moses, and Eleazar the priest, and all the princes of the congregation, went out to meet them outside of the camp.

Num 31:14 *Moses was angry with the officers of the army, the captains of thousands and the captains of hundreds, who came from the service of the war.*

Num 31:15 Moses said to them, "Have you saved all the women alive?

MY NOTES

page 112

Num 31:16 Behold, these caused the children of Israel, through the counsel of Balaam, to commit trespass against YHWH in the matter of Peor, and so the plague was among the congregation of YHWH.

Num 31:17 Now therefore kill every male among the little ones, and kill every woman who has known man by lying with him.

Num 31:18 But all the girls, who have not known man by lying with him, keep alive for yourselves.

Num 31:19 "Encamp outside of the camp for seven days. Whoever has killed any person, and whoever has touched any slain, purify yourselves on the third day and on the seventh day, you and your captives.

Num 31:20 As to every garment, and all that is made of skin, and all work of goats' hair, and all things made of wood, you shall purify yourselves."

Num 31:21 Eleazar the priest said to the men of war who went to the battle, "This is the statute of the law which YHWH has commanded Moses:

Num 31:22 however the gold, and the silver, the brass, the iron, the tin, and the lead,

Num 31:23 everything that may withstand the fire, you shall make to go through the fire, and it shall be clean; nevertheless it shall be purified with the water for impurity. All that doesn't withstand the fire you shall make to go through the water.

Num 31:24 You shall wash your clothes on the seventh day, and you shall be clean. Afterward you shall come into the camp."

WEDNESDAY Num 31:25 YHWH spoke to Moses, saying,

Num 31:26 "Count the plunder that was taken, both of man and of animal, you, and Eleazar the priest, and the heads of the fathers' households of the congregation;

Num 31:27 and divide the plunder into two parts: between the men skilled in war, who went out to battle, and all the congregation.

Num 31:28 Levy a tribute to YHWH of the men of war who went out to battle: one soul of five hundred; of the persons, of the cattle, of the donkeys, and of the flocks.

Num 31:29 Take it from their half, and give it to Eleazar the priest, for YHWH's wave offering.

Num 31:30 *Of the children of Israel's half, you shall take one drawn out of every fifty, of the persons, of the cattle, of the donkeys, and of the flocks, of all the livestock, and give them to the Levites, who perform the duty of YHWH's tabernacle."*

Num 31:31 Moses and Eleazar the priest did as YHWH commanded Moses.

MY NOTES

Num 31:32 Now the plunder, over and above the booty which the men of war took, was six hundred seventy-five thousand sheep,

Num 31:33 and seventy-two thousand head of cattle,

Num 31:34 and sixty-one thousand donkeys,

Num 31:35 and thirty-two thousand persons in all, of the women who had not known man by lying with him.

Num 31:36 The half, which was the portion of those who went out to war, was in number three hundred thirty-seven thousand five hundred sheep:

Num 31:37 and YHWH's tribute of the sheep was six hundred seventy-five.

Num 31:38 The cattle were thirty-six thousand; of which YHWH's tribute was seventy-two.

Num 31:39 The donkeys were thirty thousand five hundred; of which YHWH's tribute was sixty-one.

Num 31:40 The persons were sixteen thousand; of whom YHWH's tribute was thirty-two persons.

Num 31:41 Moses gave the tribute, which was YHWH's wave offering, to Eleazar the priest, as YHWH commanded Moses.

THURSDAY Num 31:42 Of the children of Israel's half, which Moses divided off from the men who fought

Num 31:43 (now the congregation's half was three hundred thirty-seven thousand five hundred sheep,

Num 31:44 and thirty-six thousand head of cattle,

Num 31:45 and thirty thousand five hundred donkeys,

Num 31:46 and sixteen thousand persons),

Num 31:47 even of the children of Israel's half, Moses took one drawn out of every fifty, both of man and of animal, and gave them to the Levites, who performed the duty of YHWH's tabernacle; as YHWH commanded Moses.

Num 31:48 The officers who were over the thousands of the army, the captains of thousands, and the captains of hundreds, came near to Moses.

Num 31:49 They said to Moses, "Your servants have taken the sum of the men of war who are under our command, and there lacks not one man of us.

Num 31:50 We have brought YHWH's offering, what every man found: gold ornaments, armlets, bracelets, signet rings, earrings, and necklaces, to make atonement for our souls before YHWH."

Num 31:51 Moses and Eleazar the priest took their gold, even all worked jewels.

MY NOTES

Num 31:52 All the gold of the wave offering that they offered up to YHWH, of the captains of thousands, and of the captains of hundreds, was sixteen thousand seven hundred fifty shekels.

Num 31:53 The men of war had taken booty, every man for himself.

Num 31:54 Moses and Eleazar the priest took the gold of the captains of thousands and of hundreds, and brought it into the Tent of Meeting, for a memorial for the children of Israel before YHWH.

Reuben and Gad Settle in Gilead

FRIDAY Num 32:1 Now the children of Reuben and the children of Gad had a very great multitude of livestock. They saw the land of Jazer, and the land of Gilead. Behold, the place was a place for livestock.

Num 32:2 Then the children of Gad and the children of Reuben came and spoke to Moses, and to Eleazar the priest, and to the princes of the congregation, saying,

Num 32:3 "Ataroth, Dibon, Jazer, Nimrah, Heshbon, Elealeh, Sebam, Nebo, and Beon,

Num 32:4 the land which YHWH struck before the congregation of Israel, is a land for livestock; and your servants have livestock."

Num 32:5 They said, "If we have found favor in your sight, let this land be given to your servants for a possession. Don't bring us over the Jordan."

Num 32:6 Moses said to the children of Gad, and to the children of Reuben, "Shall your brothers go to war while you sit here?

Num 32:7 Why do you discourage the heart of the children of Israel from going over into the land which YHWH has given them?

Num 32:8 Your fathers did so when I sent them from Kadesh Barnea to see the land.

Num 32:9 For when they went up to the valley of Eshcol, and saw the land, they discouraged the heart of the children of Israel, that they should not go into the land which YHWH had given them.

Num 32:10 YHWH's anger burned in that day, and he swore, saying,

Num 32:11 'Surely none of the men who came up out of Egypt, from twenty years old and upward, shall see the land which I swore to Abraham, to Isaac, and to Jacob; because they have not wholly followed me,

Num 32:12 except Caleb the son of Jephunneh the Kenizzite, and Joshua the son of Nun; because they have followed YHWH completely.'

MY NOTES

Num 32:13 *YHWH's anger burned against Israel, and he made them wander back and forth in the wilderness forty years, until all the generation, who had done evil in YHWH's sight, was consumed.*

Num 32:14 "Behold, you have risen up in your fathers' place, an increase of sinful men, to increase the fierce anger of YHWH toward Israel.

Num 32:15 For if you turn away from after him, he will yet again leave them in the wilderness; and you will destroy all these people."

Num 32:16 They came near to him, and said, "We will build sheepfolds here for our livestock, and cities for our little ones;

Num 32:17 but we ourselves will be ready armed to go before the children of Israel, until we have brought them to their place. Our little ones shall dwell in the fortified cities because of the inhabitants of the land.

Num 32:18 We will not return to our houses until the children of Israel have all received their inheritance.

Num 32:19 For we will not inherit with them on the other side of the Jordan and beyond; because our inheritance has come to us on this side of the Jordan eastward."

SABBATH Num 32:20 Moses said to them, "If you will do this thing, if you will arm yourselves to go before YHWH to the war,

Num 32:21 and every one of your armed men will pass over the Jordan before YHWH, until he has driven out his enemies from before him,

Num 32:22 and the land is subdued before YHWH; then afterward you shall return, and be clear of obligation to YHWH and to Israel. Then this land shall be your possession before YHWH.

Num 32:23 *"But if you will not do so, behold, you have sinned against YHWH; and be sure your sin will find you out.*

Num 32:24 Build cities for your little ones, and folds for your sheep; and do that which has proceeded out of your mouth."

Num 32:25 The children of Gad and the children of Reuben spoke to Moses, saying, "Your servants will do as my lord commands.

Num 32:26 Our little ones, our wives, our flocks, and all our livestock, shall be there in the cities of Gilead;

Num 32:27 but your servants will pass over, every man who is armed for war, before YHWH to battle, as my lord says."

Num 32:28 So Moses commanded concerning them to Eleazar the priest, and to Joshua the son of Nun, and to the heads of the fathers' households of the tribes of the children of Israel.

MY NOTES

Num 32:29 Moses said to them, "If the children of Gad and the children of Reuben will pass with you over the Jordan, every man who is armed to battle, before YHWH, and the land is subdued before you, then you shall give them the land of Gilead for a possession;

Num 32:30 but if they will not pass over with you armed, they shall have possessions among you in the land of Canaan."

Num 32:31 The children of Gad and the children of Reuben answered, saying, "As YHWH has said to your servants, so will we do.

Num 32:32 We will pass over armed before YHWH into the land of Canaan, and the possession of our inheritance shall remain with us beyond the Jordan."

Num 32:33 Moses gave to them, even to the children of Gad, and to the children of Reuben, and to the half-tribe of Manasseh the son of Joseph, the kingdom of Sihon king of the Amorites, and the kingdom of Og king of Bashan, the land, according to its cities and borders, even the cities of the surrounding land.

Num 32:34 The children of Gad built Dibon, Ataroth, Aroer,

Num 32:35 Atrothshophan, Jazer, Jogbehah,

Num 32:36 Beth Nimrah, and Beth Haran: fortified cities, and folds for sheep.

Num 32:37 The children of Reuben built Heshbon, Elealeh, Kiriathaim,

Num 32:38 Nebo, and Baal Meon, (their names being changed), and Sibmah. They gave other names to the cities which they built.

Num 32:39 The children of Machir the son of Manasseh went to Gilead, took it, and dispossessed the Amorites who were therein.

Num 32:40 Moses gave Gilead to Machir the son of Manasseh; and he lived therein.

Num 32:41 Jair the son of Manasseh went and took its villages, and called them Havvoth Jair.

Num 32:42 Nobah went and took Kenath, and its villages, and called it Nobah, after his own name.

MY NOTES

CRYPTOGRAM – Matthew 5:37

A	B	C	D	E	F	G	H	I	J	K	L	M	N	O	P	Q	R	S	T	U	V	W	X	Y	Z
				4			18						12							23	19		17		

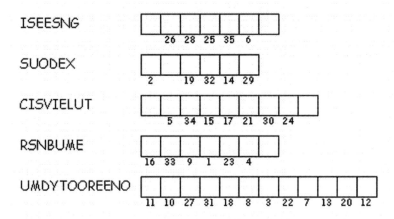

```
      E       Y O        ' Y E  '    E    ' Y E  '
 5 13 2   22 4 2   17 12 13 14   17 4 9   5 4   17 4 9

       Y O        '  O ' E  '  O .'  W          E V E
3 11 21  17 12 13 14   11 12   5 4   11 12   19 25 3 2 4 23 4 14

 I   O   E              E   E I   O       E
18 9  10 12 14 4   2 25 3 11  2 25 4 9 4   18 9   12 26   2 25 4

      E V I   O   E .
   4 23 18 22   12 11 4
```

VERSEFIND – JEREMIAH 1:5

ISEESNG
```
26 28 25 35 6
```

SUODEX
```
2    19 32 14 29
```

CISVIELUT
```
5 34 15 17 21 30 24
```

RSNBUME
```
16 33 9 1 23 4
```

UMDYTOOREENO
```
11 10 27 31 18 8 3 22 7 13 20 12
```

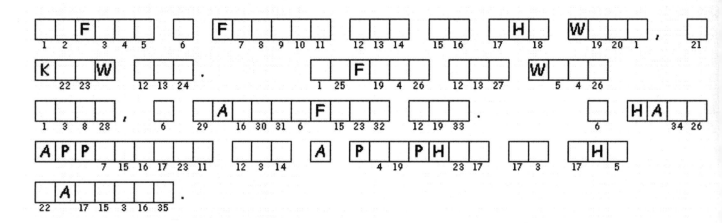

```
  F                F              H    W    ,
1 2   3 4 5   6   7 8 9 10 11   12 13 14   15 16   17   18   19 20 1   21

K   W          .           F              W
22 23   12 13 24       1 25 19 4 26   12 13 27   5 4 26

        ,       A       F         .        H A
1 3 8 28   6   29 16 30 31 6   15 23 32   12 19 33   6   34 26

A P P              A   P   P H          H
   7 15 16 17 23 11   12 3 14   4 19   23 17   17 3   17 5

  A        .
22 17 15 3 16 35
```

page 118

MASEI

מַסְעֵי

NUMBERS

It Means: JOURNEYS

Our Forty-Third Torah Portion is called Masei! מַסְעֵי
Numbers 33:1 – Numbers 36:13
PROPHETS: Jeremiah 2:4-28; 3:4
NEW TESTAMENT: Matthew 24:1-25:46; Philippians 3:7-21; James 4:1-12

MAKE A MARK
Each time you hear someone say one of the words below make a '/" beside the word. See how many marks you can get!

Moses	
promise	
years	
new	
Joshua	
died	

FIRST FIND
~

If someone mentions a verse or scripture that is NOT in this Torah Portion, see if YOU can be the First to Find it!

This Weeks Torah Portion is:

Parsha: _____

Scriptures: _____

Name: _____

words I didn't Understand

?!

My Favorite Song was:

date: _____

I talked to _____
about Today's Study.

The Most IMPORTANT thing I Learned today was:

MY NOTES

Draw something you learned today

I brought My Bible with me
I am sitting with my Family
I am ready to listen Carefully

Recounting Israel's Journey

SUNDAY Num 33:1 These are the journeys of the children of Israel, when they went out of the land of Egypt by their armies under the hand of Moses and Aaron.

Num 33:2 *Moses wrote the starting points of their journeys by the commandment of YHWH. These are their journeys according to their starting points.*

Num 33:3 They traveled from Rameses in the first month, on the fifteenth day of the first month; on the next day after the Passover, the children of Israel went out with a high hand in the sight of all the Egyptians,

Num 33:4 while the Egyptians were burying all their firstborn, whom YHWH had struck among them. YHWH also executed judgments on their gods.

Num 33:5 The children of Israel traveled from Rameses, and encamped in Succoth.

Num 33:6 They traveled from Succoth, and encamped in Etham, which is in the edge of the wilderness.

Num 33:7 They traveled from Etham, and turned back to Pihahiroth, which is before Baal Zephon: and they encamped before Migdol.

Num 33:8 They traveled from before Hahiroth, and crossed through the middle of the sea into the wilderness. They went three days' journey in the wilderness of Etham, and encamped in Marah.

Num 33:9 They traveled from Marah, and came to Elim. In Elim, there were twelve springs of water, and seventy palm trees; and they encamped there.

Num 33:10 They traveled from Elim, and encamped by the Red Sea.

MONDAY Num 33:11 *They traveled from the Red Sea, and encamped in the wilderness of Sin.*

Num 33:12 They traveled from the wilderness of Sin, and encamped in Dophkah.

Num 33:13 They traveled from Dophkah, and encamped in Alush.

Num 33:14 They traveled from Alush, and encamped in Rephidim, where there was no water for the people to drink.

Num 33:15 They traveled from Rephidim, and encamped in the wilderness of Sinai.

Num 33:16 They traveled from the wilderness of Sinai, and encamped in Kibroth Hattaavah.

Num 33:17 They traveled from Kibroth Hattaavah, and encamped in Hazeroth.

Num 33:18 They traveled from Hazeroth, and encamped in Rithmah.

Num 33:19 They traveled from Rithmah, and encamped in Rimmon Perez.

Num 33:20 They traveled from Rimmon Perez, and encamped in Libnah.

Num 33:21 They traveled from Libnah, and encamped in Rissah.

Num 33:22 They traveled from Rissah, and encamped in Kehelathah.

Num 33:23 They traveled from Kehelathah, and encamped in Mount Shepher.

Num 33:24 They traveled from Mount Shepher, and encamped in Haradah.

Num 33:25 They traveled from Haradah, and encamped in Makheloth.

Num 33:26 They traveled from Makheloth, and encamped in Tahath.

Num 33:27 They traveled from Tahath, and encamped in Terah.

Num 33:28 They traveled from Terah, and encamped in Mithkah.

Num 33:29 They traveled from Mithkah, and encamped in Hashmonah.

Num 33:30 They traveled from Hashmonah, and encamped in Moseroth.

Num 33:31 They traveled from Moseroth, and encamped in Bene Jaakan.

Num 33:32 They traveled from Bene Jaakan, and encamped in Hor Haggidgad.

Num 33:33 They traveled from Hor Haggidgad, and encamped in Jotbathah.

Num 33:34 They traveled from Jotbathah, and encamped in Abronah.

Num 33:35 They traveled from Abronah, and encamped in Ezion Geber.

Num 33:36 They traveled from Ezion Geber, and encamped at Kadesh in the wilderness of Zin.

Num 33:37 They traveled from Kadesh, and encamped in Mount Hor, in the edge of the land of Edom.

Num 33:38 Aaron the priest went up into Mount Hor at the commandment of YHWH, and died there, in the fortieth year after the children of Israel had come out of the land of Egypt, in the fifth month, on the first day of the month.

MY NOTES

Num 33:39 Aaron was one hundred twenty-three years old when he died in Mount Hor.

Num 33:40 The Canaanite, the king of Arad, who lived in the South in the land of Canaan, heard of the coming of the children of Israel.

Num 33:41 They traveled from Mount Hor, and encamped in Zalmonah.

Num 33:42 They traveled from Zalmonah, and encamped in Punon.

Num 33:43 They traveled from Punon, and encamped in Oboth.

Num 33:44 They traveled from Oboth, and encamped in Iye Abarim, in the border of Moab.

Num 33:45 They traveled from Iyim, and encamped in Dibon Gad.

Num 33:46 They traveled from Dibon Gad, and encamped in Almon Diblathaim.

Num 33:47 They traveled from Almon Diblathaim, and encamped in the mountains of Abarim, before Nebo.

Num 33:48 They traveled from the mountains of Abarim, and encamped in the plains of Moab by the Jordan at Jericho.

Num 33:49 They encamped by the Jordan, from Beth Jeshimoth even to Abel Shittim in the plains of Moab.

Drive Out the Inhabitants

TUESDAY Num 33:50 YHWH spoke to Moses in the plains of Moab by the Jordan at Jericho, saying,

Num 33:51 Speak to the children of Israel, and tell them, "When you pass over the Jordan into the land of Canaan,

Num 33:52 then you shall drive out all the inhabitants of the land from before you, destroy all their stone idols, destroy all their molten images, and demolish all their high places.

Num 33:53 *You shall take possession of the land, and dwell therein; for I have given the land to you to possess it.*

Num 33:54 You shall inherit the land by lot according to your families; to the more you shall give the more inheritance, and to the fewer you shall give the less inheritance. Wherever the lot falls to any man, that shall be his. You shall inherit according to the tribes of your fathers.

Num 33:55 "But if you do not drive out the inhabitants of the land from before you, then those you let remain of them will be like pricks in your eyes and thorns in your sides. They will harass you in the land in which you dwell.

Num 33:56 It shall happen that as I thought to do to them, so I will do to you."

MY NOTES

Boundaries of the Land

Num 34:1 YHWH spoke to Moses, saying,

Num 34:2 "Command the children of Israel, and tell them, 'When you come into the land of Canaan (this is the land that shall fall to you for an inheritance, even the land of Canaan according to its borders),

Num 34:3 then your south quarter shall be from the wilderness of Zin along by the side of Edom, and your south border shall be from the end of the Salt Sea eastward.

Num 34:4 Your border shall turn about southward of the ascent of Akrabbim, and pass along to Zin; and it shall pass southward of Kadesh Barnea; and it shall go from there to Hazar Addar, and pass along to Azmon.

Num 34:5 The border shall turn about from Azmon to the brook of Egypt, and it shall end at the sea.

Num 34:6 "'For the western border, you shall have the great sea and its border. This shall be your west border.

Num 34:7 "'This shall be your north border: from the great sea you shall mark out for yourselves Mount Hor.

Num 34:8 From Mount Hor you shall mark out to the entrance of Hamath; and the border shall pass by Zedad.

Num 34:9 Then the border shall go to Ziphron, and it shall end at Hazar Enan. This shall be your north border.

Num 34:10 "'You shall mark out your east border from Hazar Enan to Shepham.

Num 34:11 The border shall go down from Shepham to Riblah, on the east side of Ain. The border shall go down, and shall reach to the side of the sea of Chinnereth eastward.

Num 34:12 The border shall go down to the Jordan, and end at the Salt Sea. This shall be your land according to its borders around it.'"

Num 34:13 Moses commanded the children of Israel, saying, "This is the land which you shall inherit by lot, which YHWH has commanded to give to the nine tribes, and to the half-tribe;

Num 34:14 for the tribe of the children of Reuben according to their fathers' houses, the tribe of the children of Gad according to their fathers' houses, and the half-tribe of Manasseh have received their inheritance.

Num 34:15 The two tribes and the half-tribe have received their inheritance beyond the Jordan at Jericho eastward, toward the sunrise."

MY NOTES

List of Tribal Chiefs

WEDNESDAY Num 34:16 YHWH spoke to Moses, saying,

Num 34:17 "These are the names of the men who shall divide the land to you for inheritance: Eleazar the priest, and Joshua the son of Nun.

Num 34:18 **You shall take one prince of every tribe, to divide the land for inheritance.**

Num 34:19 These are the names of the men: Of the tribe of Judah, Caleb the son of Jephunneh.

Num 34:20 Of the tribe of the children of Simeon, Shemuel the son of Ammihud.

Num 34:21 Of the tribe of Benjamin, Elidad the son of Chislon.

Num 34:22 Of the tribe of the children of Dan a prince, Bukki the son of Jogli.

Num 34:23 Of the children of Joseph: of the tribe of the children of Manasseh a prince, Hanniel the son of Ephod.

Num 34:24 Of the tribe of the children of Ephraim a prince, Kemuel the son of Shiphtan.

Num 34:25 Of the tribe of the children of Zebulun a prince, Elizaphan the son of Parnach.

Num 34:26 Of the tribe of the children of Issachar a prince, Paltiel the son of Azzan.

Num 34:27 Of the tribe of the children of Asher a prince, Ahihud the son of Shelomi.

Num 34:28 Of the tribe of the children of Naphtali a prince, Pedahel the son of Ammihud."

Num 34:29 These are they whom YHWH commanded to divide the inheritance to the children of Israel in the land of Canaan.

Cities for the Levites

THURSDAY Num 35:1 YHWH spoke to Moses in the plains of Moab by the Jordan at Jericho, saying,

Num 35:2 **"Command the children of Israel to give to the Levites cities to dwell in out of their inheritance. You shall give pasture lands for the cities around them to the Levites.**

Num 35:3 They shall have the cities to dwell in. Their pasture lands shall be for their livestock, and for their possessions, and for all their animals.

Num 35:4 "The pasture lands of the cities, which you shall give to the Levites, shall be from the wall of the city and outward one thousand cubits around it.

Num 35:5 You shall measure outside of the city for the east side two thousand cubits, and for the south side two thousand cubits, and for the west side two thousand cubits, and for the north side two thousand cubits, the city being in the middle. This shall be the pasture lands of their cities.

Num 35:6 "The cities which you shall give to the Levites, they shall be the six cities of refuge, which you shall give for the man slayer to flee to. Besides them you shall give forty-two cities.

Num 35:7 All the cities which you shall give to the Levites shall be forty-eight cities together with their pasture lands.

Num 35:8 Concerning the cities which you shall give of the possession of the children of Israel, from the many you shall take many; and from the few you shall take few. Everyone according to his inheritance which he inherits shall give some of his cities to the Levites."

Cities of Refuge

FRIDAY Num 35:9 YHWH spoke to Moses, saying,

Num 35:10 "Speak to the children of Israel, and tell them, 'When you pass over the Jordan into the land of Canaan,

Num 35:11 *then you shall appoint for yourselves cities to be cities of refuge for you, that the man slayer who kills any person unwittingly may flee there.*

Num 35:12 The cities shall be for your refuge from the avenger, that the man slayer not die, until he stands before the congregation for judgment.

Num 35:13 The cities which you shall give shall be for you six cities of refuge.

Num 35:14 You shall give three cities beyond the Jordan, and you shall give three cities in the land of Canaan. They shall be cities of refuge.

Num 35:15 For the children of Israel, and for the stranger and for the foreigner living among them, shall these six cities be for refuge; that everyone who kills any person unwittingly may flee there.

Num 35:16 "'But if he struck him with an instrument of iron, so that he died, he is a murderer. The murderer shall surely be put to death.

Num 35:17 If he struck him with a stone in the hand, by which a man may die, and he died, he is a murderer. The murderer shall surely be put to death.

Num 35:18 Or if he struck him with a weapon of wood in the hand, by which a man may die, and he died, he is a murderer. The murderer shall surely be put to death.

Num 35:19 The avenger of blood shall himself put the murderer to death. When he meets him, he shall put him to death.

Num 35:5 You shall measure outside of the city for the east side two thousand cubits, and for the south side two thousand cubits, and for the west side two thousand cubits, and for the north side two thousand cubits, the city being in the middle. This shall be the pasture lands of their cities.

Num 35:6 "The cities which you shall give to the Levites, they shall be the six cities of refuge, which you shall give for the man slayer to flee to. Besides them you shall give forty-two cities.

Num 35:7 All the cities which you shall give to the Levites shall be forty-eight cities together with their pasture lands.

Num 35:8 Concerning the cities which you shall give of the possession of the children of Israel, from the many you shall take many; and from the few you shall take few. Everyone according to his inheritance which he inherits shall give some of his cities to the Levites."

Cities of Refuge

FRIDAY Num 35:9 YHWH spoke to Moses, saying,

Num 35:10 "Speak to the children of Israel, and tell them, 'When you pass over the Jordan into the land of Canaan,

Num 35:11 **then you shall appoint for yourselves cities to be cities of refuge for you, that the man slayer who kills any person unwittingly may flee there.**

Num 35:12 The cities shall be for your refuge from the avenger, that the man slayer not die, until he stands before the congregation for judgment.

Num 35:13 The cities which you shall give shall be for you six cities of refuge.

Num 35:14 You shall give three cities beyond the Jordan, and you shall give three cities in the land of Canaan. They shall be cities of refuge.

Num 35:15 For the children of Israel, and for the stranger and for the foreigner living among them, shall these six cities be for refuge; that everyone who kills any person unwittingly may flee there.

Num 35:16 "'But if he struck him with an instrument of iron, so that he died, he is a murderer. The murderer shall surely be put to death.

Num 35:17 If he struck him with a stone in the hand, by which a man may die, and he died, he is a murderer. The murderer shall surely be put to death.

Num 35:18 Or if he struck him with a weapon of wood in the hand, by which a man may die, and he died, he is a murderer. The murderer shall surely be put to death.

Num 35:19 The avenger of blood shall himself put the murderer to death. When he meets him, he shall put him to death.

Num 35:20 If he shoved him out of hatred, or hurled something at him, lying in wait, so that he died,

Num 35:21 or in hostility struck him with his hand, so that he died, he who struck him shall surely be put to death. He is a murderer. The avenger of blood shall put the murderer to death, when he meets him.

Num 35:22 "'But if he shoved him suddenly without hostility, or hurled on him anything without lying in wait,

Num 35:23 or with any stone, by which a man may die, not seeing him, and cast it on him, so that he died, and he was not his enemy, neither sought his harm;

Num 35:24 then the congregation shall judge between the striker and the avenger of blood according to these ordinances.

Num 35:25 The congregation shall deliver the man slayer out of the hand of the avenger of blood, and the congregation shall restore him to his city of refuge, where he had fled. He shall dwell therein until the death of the high priest, who was anointed with the holy oil.

Num 35:26 "'But if the man slayer shall at any time go beyond the border of his city of refuge, where he flees,

Num 35:27 and the avenger of blood finds him outside of the border of his city of refuge, and the avenger of blood kills the man slayer; he shall not be guilty of blood,

Num 35:28 because he should have remained in his city of refuge until the death of the high priest. But after the death of the high priest, the man slayer shall return into the land of his possession.

Num 35:29 "'These things shall be for a statute and ordinance to you throughout your generations in all your dwellings.

Num 35:30 "'Whoever kills any person, the murderer shall be slain based on the testimony of witnesses; but one witness shall not testify alone against any person so that he dies.

Num 35:31 "'Moreover you shall take no ransom for the life of a murderer who is guilty of death. He shall surely be put to death.

Num 35:32 "'You shall take no ransom for him who has fled to his city of refuge, that he may come again to dwell in the land, until after the death of the priest.

Num 35:33 "'So you shall not pollute the land where you live; for blood pollutes the land. No atonement can be made for the land, for the blood that is shed in it, but by the blood of him who shed it.

Num 35:34 You shall not defile the land which you inhabit, where I dwell; for I, YHWH, dwell among the children of Israel.'"

MY NOTES

page 129

Marriage of Female Heirs

SABBATH Num 36:1 The heads of the fathers' households of the family of the children of Gilead, the son of Machir, the son of Manasseh, of the families of the sons of Joseph, came near, and spoke before Moses, and before the princes, the heads of the fathers' households of the children of Israel.

Num 36:2 They said, "YHWH commanded my lord to give the land for inheritance by lot to the children of Israel. My lord was commanded by YHWH to give the inheritance of Zelophehad our brother to his daughters.

Num 36:3 If they are married to any of the sons of the other tribes of the children of Israel, then their inheritance will be taken away from the inheritance of our fathers, and will be added to the inheritance of the tribe to which they shall belong. So it will be taken away from the lot of our inheritance.

Num 36:4 ***When the jubilee of the children of Israel comes, then their inheritance will be added to the inheritance of the tribe to which they shall belong. So their inheritance will be taken away from the inheritance of the tribe of our fathers.***"

Num 36:5 Moses commanded the children of Israel according to YHWH's word, saying, "The tribe of the sons of Joseph speak what is right.

Num 36:6 This is the thing which YHWH commands concerning the daughters of Zelophehad, saying, 'Let them be married to whom they think best; only they shall marry into the family of the tribe of their father.

Num 36:7 So shall no inheritance of the children of Israel move from tribe to tribe; for the children of Israel shall all keep the inheritance of the tribe of his fathers.

Num 36:8 Every daughter who possesses an inheritance in any tribe of the children of Israel shall be wife to one of the family of the tribe of her father, that the children of Israel may each possess the inheritance of his fathers.

Num 36:9 So shall no inheritance move from one tribe to another tribe; for the tribes of the children of Israel shall each keep his own inheritance.'"

Num 36:10 The daughters of Zelophehad did as YHWH commanded Moses:

Num 36:11 for Mahlah, Tirzah, Hoglah, Milcah, and Noah, the daughters of Zelophehad, were married to their father's brothers' sons.

Num 36:12 They were married into the families of the sons of Manasseh the son of Joseph. Their inheritance remained in the tribe of the family of their father.

Num 36:13 These are the commandments and the ordinances which YHWH commanded by Moses to the children of Israel in the plains of Moab by the Jordan at Jericho.

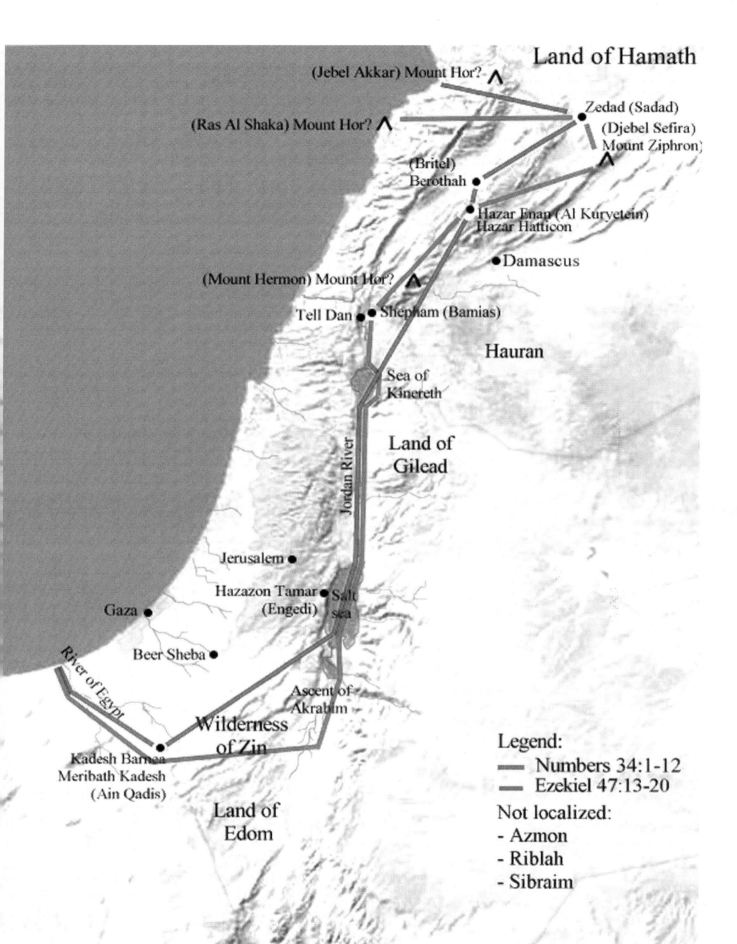

Land of Hamath

(Jebel Akkar) Mount Hor? ∧

Zedad (Sadad)

(Djebel Sefira)
Mount Ziphron) ∧

(Ras Al Shaka) Mount Hor? ∧

(Britel)
Berothah

Hazar Enan (Al Kuryetein)
Hazar Hatticon

Damascus

(Mount Hermon) Mount Hor? ∧

Tell Dan ● ● Shepham (Bamias)

Hauran

Sea of
Kinereth

Jordan River

Land of
Gilead

Jerusalem ●

Hazazon Tamar ● Salt
(Engedi) sea

Gaza ●

Beer Sheba ●

River of Egypt

Ascent of
Akrabim

Wilderness
of Zin

Kadesh Barnea
Meribath Kadesh
(Ain Qadis)

Land of
Edom

Legend:
━━ Numbers 34:1-12
━━ Ezekiel 47:13-20
Not localized:
- Azmon
- Riblah
- Sibraim

VERSE FIND - PHILIPPIANS 3:14

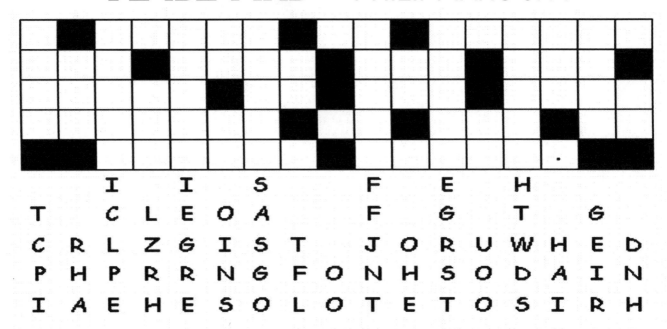

```
        I   I   S       F   E       H
T   C   L   E   O   A   F   G   T   G
C   R   L   Z   G   I   S   T   J   O   R   U   W   H   E   D
P   H   P   R   R   N   G   F   O   N   H   S   O   D   A   I   N
I   A   E   H   E   S   O   L   O   T   E   T   O   S   I   R   H
```

FILL-IN THE VERSE - JAMES 4:11

Don't speak _____ one another, brothers. He who speaks _____ a brother and _____ his brother, _____ against the law and judges the law. But if you _____ the law, you are not a doer of the law, but a _____.

PHILIPPIANS 3:20- SCRAMBLE

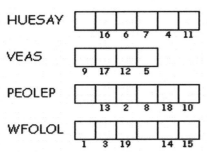

HUESAY □□□□□□
        16 6 7 4 11

VEAS   □□□□
        9 17 12 5

PEOLEP □□□□□□
        13 2 8 18 10

WFOLOL □□□□□□
        1 3 19   14 15

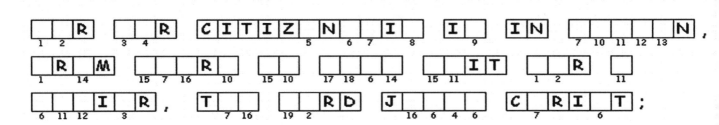

```
□ R □ □ R □ C I T I Z □ N □ I □ I □ I N □ □ □ □ □ N ,
1 2     3 4         5     6 7   8       9         7 10 11 12 13

□ R □ M □ □ R □ □ □ □ □ □ □ □ □ I T □ □ R □ □
1 14    15 7 16   10   15 10   17 18  6 14 15 11   1  2    11

□ □ □ I □ R , T □ □ □ R D □ J □ □ □ □ □ C □ R I □ T ;
6 11 12   3     7 16 19  2       16  6  4  6      7    6
```

Once again, we pray that this booklet will be a blessing to you and your children and that your children will be a blessing to others.

If you have been blessed by this ministry, please consider donating to TORAH TOWN. Please continue to keep us in your prayers as we continue to pray for you.

FACEBOOK: https://facebook.com/TorahTown
YOUTUBE: https://youtube.com/TorahTown
WEBSITE: http://torahtown.xyz

DONATIONS https://paypal.me/TorahTown

Made in the USA
Columbia, SC
18 August 2018